Messages from a Transcendent Dimension
1943 – 1965

Anne Baring

ARCHIVE
publishing

First published in the United Kingdom by
Archive Publishing
Shaftesbury, Dorset, England

Designed at Archive Publishing by Ian Thorp MA

A CIP catalogue record for this book is available from
The British Library

ISBN 978-1-906289-63-8 (Hardcase)

Front cover: '*Rose*'
from an original photograph by Kate Genevieve.

Frontispiece: '*Grail with Roses*'
from an original woodcut by Thalia Gage, inspired by the Messages.

www.archivepublishing.co.uk

Printed and bound in England by CMP (UK) Ltd.

Introduction

One winter afternoon in New York, February 1943, at the height of the Second World War, my mother, her sister, her sister-in-law, and a close friend, met to talk about the life-and-death struggle that was tearing Europe apart. (My father was serving under General Montgomery, in North Africa). Suddenly, although the windows of the apartment were closed because of the cold, they heard a roar like thunder and the glass door onto the terrace was blown inwards by a powerful blast of air. Lightning flickered all around them although there was no storm. They cried out in terror, and went to shut the door, but suddenly felt a tremendous presence in the room and, falling on their knees, were overcome with awe. Then they heard a voice which told them to write down what they heard.

The voice said: "Be sure of thy spirit as I am the wine and the bread of the One who is above the Fire and the Light and Foremost." It warned of a future catastrophe for the Earth and humanity if the ways of men did not change and said that this warning should be passed on to anyone who was willing to listen. If enough people could become aware of the danger and respond to the guidance that was trying to reach them, the full force of the catastrophe could be mitigated or even averted.

Filled with grief over the war in Europe, my mother found the courage to ask what they could do to help the suffering world. When should they pray? The answer came: "Pray at the hour of the despair of the Son of Man." Should they pray in church? "Your church is your immortal soul." They were told to follow the guidance of their hearts. Only through making space in their lives for listening to the guidance that was trying to reach them from another dimension of reality could they come to a deeper understanding of how they could most effectively help the world. They learned that they were being contacted because they had once been part of the group of women who were close to Jesus during His Mission.

My mother and her friend continued to meet for some twenty-five years to receive further messages. (Her sister moved to another country and her sister-in-law was tragically killed in Italy at the end of the war). The messages warned (in 1944) of the dangers of splitting the atom and interfering with the laws of Nature because of the disintegrative effects this would have on the human psyche and the life of the planet in general. They said that because of the splitting of the atom, each of us was now our brother's keeper. They also told them to study the early history of Christianity, the twelfth and thirteenth centuries and the Reformation. They were to study how the teaching of Jesus had been distorted or obscured by the Church established in His name. Repeatedly they were urged to follow the thread of guidance that would lead them to something called the 'Dream of the Water', and to find their way to the 'Holy Mountain'. They were also told to look for a mysterious stone 'buried at the foot of the Tree'.

At first my mother and her friend took these images literally and looked for a place of refuge from the impending catastrophe (whose date was never specified), even spending some time searching for a holy mountain and a tree under which a special stone might be buried. Gradually, it dawned on them that these images were not to be understood literally but were metaphors for a state of being or state of consciousness which they needed to develop within them.

They were told to listen and only to write when the voice was clear. They were sent to the holy places of Europe and beyond, not always together as their lives made it difficult for them to leave their obligations at the same time. But they were told to create links between these places — patterns of light to create a golden web: the triangle of Glastonbury, Mont Saint Michel and Iona; The Aliscamps at Arles with Monte Gargano in southern Italy and Chartres in the north of France; Monségur in south-western France with Montserrat in Spain and Mont Saint Victoire in Provence; Arunachala in southern India with Mounts Kailas and Everest; Ephesus with Pergamum and Crete.

The angel of Chartres appeared to them on the 14th of April, 1943: "I am born of the fire and I protect. Kneel and pray. The Master has sent me to give you comfort and consolation. Divine Love should be so strong that it eliminates the distances and abolishes the classes. The rich should help the poor and the poor will save the rich. No more prejudices and divisions because we are all the servants of God. Pray and you will be consoled. You should wait with your sisters in Christ to receive the light that once showered upon you like the dew of God."

✌❀✎

For many years they struggled to understand how these messages could be transmitted to the world of their time. Given their background and the fact that women were of no consequence in the culture of that time — the 1940's and 50's — how could they transmit to others what they had been taught? Who would listen to them? My mother, Thalia, poured her creative energy into her poetry and her paintings. Her French friend, Ninon, pursued her career as a theatre agent. They continued to meet and to receive messages for over twenty-five years. They were reluctant to believe themselves to be messengers when they knew they were not prepared or equipped for such a role. They could see no way in which the messages they had received could "fit" with their everyday lives and no way in which they could immediately rise to their level or even share them with friends. There was too big a gap between what they were asked to do and what they were able to do. So they kept them to themselves and a few close friends — all women.

I grew up with these Messages from the age of thirteen and they entered deeply into my soul. Becoming an adult, there seemed to be no way in which I could bring them to the attention of others; no way, in the predominantly materialist culture of that time, that I could even mention them without incurring disbelief and ridicule. When my mother died in 1994, I inherited the notebooks containing these messages and the world has changed sufficiently in the last thirty years (most importantly through the coming of the Internet and the growing voice of women) for me to be able to put many of them into the public domain.

In 1956, when I was twenty-five, having graduated from Oxford University in 1951, my life took an unexpected direction. I was commissioned by an Italian Encyclopaedia of Art in Rome, to travel to India and south-east Asia, to gather photographs of the greatest works of art from the museums of these different countries. These included Thailand, Burma, Cambodia, Indonesia, Taiwan and Japan. China was unfortunately out of bounds at that time. This incredible commission hugely expanded my understanding of the history and culture of these countries, introduced me to Hinduism, Buddhism and Taoism and gave me a deeper understanding of Christianity. When I returned after a year's travelling, I wrote my first book, *The One Work: A Journey Towards the Self*, in which I tried to show how these spiritual traditions carry the same essential message — the need to raise our consciousness to a higher level. [1]

However, I could not answer two questions: with all these great spiritual traditions, why was the world perpetually preparing for war? Why were we, the human species, so out of touch with Nature and the cosmos, so unconscious, that we no longer recognised the deeper reality that the world's religions had tried to connect us with? These questions and my inability to answer them, caused me to fall into a deep depression which, in turn, led me to enter Jungian Analysis and, after many years, to train as a Jungian Analyst myself. This long experience, together with a powerful visionary dream and writing a book on the Goddess, with my friend and fellow analyst, Jules Cashford, led me to answer my two questions and to write a further book which could incorporate the essence and even some of the words of the Messages. [2]

The Messages came from a transcendent dimension of the Cosmos, from Jesus (Yeshua), St. Francis and a Persian angelic guide called Asraf or Hazarat. Ninon was my mother's closest friend who, with my mother sitting next to her, wrote down the words she heard. They never doubted their authenticity. The fact that there exist higher dimensions of the universe and that the universe is peopled by multitudes of conscious beings, may be unfamiliar to many people, yet in older civilisations, their existence was known and accepted and contact with them was maintained by shamans and mystics. In the words of Chris Bache, a close friend, "We are everywhere surrounded by orders of reality beyond reckoning." [3]

Although the language in which the Messages are expressed

may seem arcane and strange to the modern reader, they were framed in such a way that their meaning was accessible to my mother and her friend. It soon became obvious that this planet was being closely watched by those who were concerned about the increasing danger it was in through the struggle for supremacy between leaders of nations who were developing ever more powerful nuclear weapons. While the concept of God as "the Father" may prove problematic to some readers, my mother and her friend would not have been able to assimilate a different concept of God as there was nothing in their experience or education that could have led them to it. I should mention that the concept of reincarnation was familiar to them, so reference to their lives two thousand years ago did not seem strange.

In the 1940's, living in Washington DC, my mother became interested in Mary Magdalene and began to research what she could discover about her life in the Library of Congress there. This led to her publishing in 1952 a prose-poem called *Prelude to Pentecost* about the life of Mary, her sister Martha and her brother Lazarus. She would have been thrilled to know about the authentic gospel of Mary Magdalene that has been recently translated (2010) from an ancient Alexandrian Greek text that had been for many centuries, the closely guarded treasure of a Cathar Community in the Languedoc area of south-western France. It is probable that it had been brought to France by Mary Magdalene herself before 50 AD. This was the very area that my mother found herself moving to in 1960, living there until the end of her life in 1994. [4] The title of this unique text was *The Gospel of the Beloved Companion*. In that gospel, she would have discovered, to her amazement and delight, that Jesus, or Yeshua (his Aramaic name), refers throughout this gospel to the Holy Spirit as his Mother, and that Mary Magdalene was his beloved wife, appointed by him teacher to the disciples just before the Last Supper. She would also have discovered the authentic message of Yeshua that has been so distorted by the Church founded in his name. This newly revealed gospel would have confirmed for her everything that the Messages she had received had tried to impart.

Now, reaching the end of my life, I would like to offer these

Messages to whoever might be interested in listening to their dire warnings and their teachings. What they transmitted to my mother and her friend in 1943, is more relevant today than it was eighty years ago since the dangers we face are far greater now. AI technology is racing ahead, urged on by the same male competitive ethos that is driving the further development of nuclear weapons, the dangerous work of gain-of-function laboratories and other technologies which harm the miraculous organism of the human body and interfere with the delicate balance of the planet's life — all involving the participation of people who do not hold the best interests of the planet at heart. Our survival demands that we relinquish the ongoing rivalry and struggle for power between nations which could destroy the Earth and ourselves with it, and choose the alternative path of love and service of the planet and all the precious orders of life it embraces.

This is a key moment in our evolutionary journey. The choices we make now will determine our future and whether there is a future. The Messages say that if we are to experience the Blessing of the Millennium, we need to end all war and killing now. Women are one half of humanity and, therefore, hold the balance at this crucial time of choice. The power of millions of women, coming together to protect this Sacred Planet, could not only eliminate war but allow us to write a New Story.

1. Gage, Anne *The One Work: A Journey Towards the Self,*
    Vincent Stuart, London, 1961
2. Baring, Anne and Cashford, Jules *The Myth of the Goddess: Evolution of an Image*, Penguin Books, London, 1992 …also
    Baring, Anne *The Dream of the Cosmos: A Quest for the Soul,*
    Archive Publishing, Shaftesbury, 2013 & 2020
3. Christopher Bache, *Dark Night, Early Dawn*, State University of New York Press, 2000
4. de Quillan, Jehanne. Translation and Commentary. *The Gospel of the Beloved Companion*, Éditions Athara, Foix, France. Available on Amazon.

❧❀☙

January 16th, 1944
Thalia, Ninon, and Lilla, a friend — through Ninon

The new world is being born in the East; the New Age is being born on the top of the mountains. This time East and West will merge into one great continent. Alleluia! Alleluia! the New Age is born!

You are on the point of starting your great journey. For all of you there is a specific place for you to go where you will receive your messages from the higher planes. From pain and chaos, the way to the Light lies before you. Be humble, ready, and aware. Make your bodies the temple of your souls. All the pillars of this temple must be decorated as for the great festivity. Be joyful, be happy, for I am with you, dancing in your souls as the sun dances in the air, the great dance of life as it awaits the eternal resurrection.

I am the Lord of Light, of the Peace which can blossom through pain, as a flower can blossom through mud and blood. You have all been with Me before and I have come to you, so be alive and joyful as from now on I will always watch over you, and be with you. You have waited for Me and I have come to you.

❧❀☙

February 29th, 1944
Thalia, Ninon and Lilla — through Ninon

Blessings on all three of you, My most beloved flock. Yes, you were already with Me at the time of My teaching in the East. You always will be with Me because you were born with the desire to serve in your heart. You have seen the evil in man. You have seen his ignorance; yet you have kept faith because you knew that all the time, I was with you and you were ready to serve.

Now My dear children, listen to Me and listen well as this is very important for you. Grievous days are ahead because never before has the force of evil tried so hard to establish its kingdom on Earth. Unexpected events will take place that will bring much pain, and cause much blood to be shed. People think they can play with the Enemy of Man but they cannot. They will have to learn this great lesson. As long as they have not learnt it, there will be blood and tears. Man is on the threshold of his greatest trials since the day of My coming and that is why I wish to help and guide all those who are expected to be the servants of the New Age that is to come after the despairing days.

My children, from now on I will be very close to you, if you will keep very close to Me, because you will need My guidance in the days to come. Meet regularly and pray every day and every night. For you, there is gladness and joy ahead. If you stay with Me, you will be conscious of the Light in the darkness, just as those who can see the stars shining in the night sky, when the skies are clouded for those who cannot see.

❧❀☙

March 3rd, 1944
Thalia, Ninon, Lilla — through Ninon

Blessings, great blessings on you, My three chosen ones. I am here with you, hovering on the edge of your thoughts as the sun hovers round the edge of the mountains. You must know that all of you will be severely tried before you will be ready to go up to your new level, which is the one of Glory, and in the protection of the Father. You have been chosen to do hard practical work as well. That is why you must be strong when the time comes. You will need all this great strength to be able to ascend to the top of the Holy Mountain and there prepare with Me the Age that is to come, when all religions will be One, and when man through woman will realise in himself the sense of his mission on Earth. He will see clearly, as in a mirror, the Law of the Universe in the Light of the Father. It will be a time, My children, when those who have reached this level, will understand the secrets of Nature and the inner meaning of life on Earth, as men now understand the wonders of science.

St. Francis, My well-beloved, will be the teacher of this New Age. That is why he has always been close to Me. In the near future, you will receive still greater revelations than those I have given you today. Be ready for them and do not let the roving spirit of Judas assail you. In the Light of the Higher Faith, pray, meditate, and let your hearts be raised in thanksgiving. Pray and ask for help and you will receive help because My love for you is infinite and knows no bounds. Pray and you will be blessed. Repeat this prayer, raising your hearts to us.

> We thank thee, the One Who is All,
> to have chosen us to be Thy servants.
> Humbly, we kneel at Thy feet,
> awaiting Thy will to come through our bodies,
>   physical and astral.
> Be our Guide, and we will follow Thee.
> When Thou speakest, we hear,
> being only Thy Incarnation
> and the grain of Thy Infinite Spirit.
>
> Love be with you.
> Love be with the world.
> Love be the only eternal blessing.

❧❀☙

April 8th, 1944
Thalia and Ninon — through Ninon

Blessings on you, children of My spoken word. This morning you were sent to a haven of peace when you could feel the blessing of peace in contrast to the destruction now raging in this miserable world.

Yes, you are the sisters of the New Age and you will have to toil for My sake, for My love, as did those who were near Me in

My earthly body. You will have to work with your hands and to travel on your knees to reach the place that has been appointed for you. You have to be strong, strong and healthy, not for the sake of material wellbeing, but for the sake of higher tasks. It is only if those, who, like you, have seen the Light and are strong enough to go on with the work, that the world can be saved.

It is the stone, buried under the grass at the foot of the tree, that has been the witness of My persecution and of your wanderings. The stone is your altar and you must go there for prayers and comfort when the days of trial come.

Upon this stone will I build My new capital. From there will start the Gospel of the New Age. It is this stone's alter being which is in the south of France where both have been at the time of your persecutions and your preaching. From there you can start to the Holy Mountain when the time comes. Go there and pray, when the moment comes, because this is your church and your holy land.

❦❦❦

August 5th, 1944
Thalia and Ninon — through Ninon

This period is the period of choice. Each soul who wants to go on has to take the decision to follow the Path, because only those who are firm in their desire to go on with the evolution of this planet will be allowed to survive materially.

The end of this Day [Age] is near. As I said at the beginning of the Age, two thousand years ago, all will have to be judged. Already, in some parts of the planet, the first signs of the end have appeared, and a liquidation has taken place. There is more to come, as I already said to you. Bells will ring, and many will rejoice, but verily there will be no cause for rejoicing. Everyone must go to the utmost depths of his soul and clean it, as the soldier does his kit, when he awaits the coming of his chief, because even we could not help you if when the moment comes you should not be as pure as the morning dew.

Do not let your minds dwell on the material aspect of the catastrophe. It will take different forms in different countries. What is important for you to know is that your period of trial is on. Those who have made the choice, are going to be measured by the measure of their choice. Their future immortality and the work they will do depends on the fulfilment of their destiny in this period of trial. Verily I say unto you that many have been chosen who have been found wanting and will not pass through the gateway.

You will hear Me more than ever when you come together in the following months as the clouds loom darker on the horizon. The blow will be sharp and violent, like thunder out of a blue sky, and it will surprise the world. The confusion will be great and it will last, as a great deal has to be atoned for before the New Age of Peace can come. The sign will come from the East and the Fire of Heaven will reveal the truth from the bowels of the earth. A time will come when the incredible will happen. It will be so unexpected, so sudden that people will totter as if they have been struck a mighty blow and are unable to believe the evidence of their eyes and ears. But those who have been warned will fall on their knees and will call to each other as birds in a storm. Those who have been warned and are prepared are still vulnerable as the enemy of man prepares many traps. But with meditation and prayer they can defeat his attacks with the steadfastness of divine faith in the purpose of God. I am praying that many can be spared.

I will not come with flames and disaster, but because of the prayers of many, who like you, believe that the Spirit of Love can conquer even the splitting elements.

Into your hands, closed on each other in firm trust, I will entrust the Light that never fails, and that will lighten all the obscurities that will be on the world at the end of these days. Pray every day and every moment when you feel doubt, fear, or sorrow. Fear is a stone in the way of your spiritual attainment. Pray and ask for help and you will receive it.

I will now lay My hands on you and give you the Blessing of My Healing Love.

❦

October 5th, 1944
Thalia and Ninon — through Ninon

Greetings, My dearly beloved daughters. You are surrounded by the blue light which you have called down upon yourselves and the white dove is over your heads. You are in the company of august presences and should bow in humble reverence at the feet of your Master who has so lovingly prepared for this meeting with three of his pupils. He was already present with you while you knelt and said the prayer, and He laid his hand upon the head of each one of you. He is ready to speak:

Love be with you, as Love is the only eternal blessing. With these words of your prayer, I greet you as I want you to have these words engraved on your souls. A time will come when the incredible will happen. It will be so incredible, so unexpected, so sudden, that people in the streets will totter as if they had been struck by a mighty blow and will not believe the evidence of their eyes and ears. But you, My dear sisters, who have been warned, will know and will fall on your knees, repeating the Blessing I gave you, calling on each other as the bird in times of storm calls for the security of its nest.

You must always have in the sight of your spiritual vision, the image of the Holy Mountain. See it capped with pure white snow with the sun striking it clearly so that it shines like the most beautiful clear-cut diamond. See it with the three of you kneeling in the snow and looking towards the sun with closed eyes. And lo, the snow will feel like soft velvet with no cold attached to it, but like warm, scented grass in the caress of spring. And at your feet will be the world, and a sadly battered world it will be, with poor demented men and women flying on every side, not knowing what has come to pass, as the unexpected has happened.

You should pray, Sisters of Love, in the purity of the Sacred Mountain, that they should be enlightened, and that the Truth passing in you, through you, for you, should be communicated to them and that they should be saved. And then you will rise with no fear in your hearts and the glad tidings on your lips, for the Valley of the Shadow will be behind, not before you.

Oh, dearest daughters, do you feel the beauty of the Mission assigned to you? Do you feel as I do that the love is uniting your consciousness to mine in a great path to the Father, whose Law you can fulfil? Let the thoughts of your everyday life be discarded as they need have no more reality for you than has the spiritual world for those who do not see. You are no more the individuals that you were; you are My chosen daughters. Though your task is to continue to take care of your everyday burdens, you must do it with the minimum of wasted energy and concentrate your force of mind and heart on preparation for your spiritual task.

I bless you, My daughters, and say unto you, be of good cheer. You will cross the desert of darkness with the light of innocence and trust to guide you, so that the darkness will not be shadow but a blue abyss of dark light which will spur you to the place of your destiny.

❦

October 18th, 1944
Thalia and Ninon — through Ninon

The Light be on you. As the Shepherd of Peace, I love you and take you to My bosom.

I want to tell you tonight that some of the secrets you are seeking will soon be made visible to you and you will see in the blue light of the cosmic radiance the scenes of your past lives that have bound you together through seven incarnations. You will see them and also be informed on what was called the Grail in past times as this is important for your own illumination. The progress you are making is bringing you closer and closer to the Sacred Mountain without your realising its vicinity. Yet it is so close that you can almost touch it, as if the hour decided upon in the course of time had already struck. But the invisible clock is getting closer and closer to the crucial time.

Watch and pray, My sisters of Love, as the journey will be strenuous and you need all your strength to tread the narrow way that leads to the top of the Mountain of the Father. You must bear in your mind the sense of your mission, which is one with that mission which I breathed unto My followers when I gave them the power to go forth into the world. Verily, verily, I say unto you, your hearts must be modest and strong and so full of the Eternal Truth that it would be easier to wrench a stone out of the depths of the deepest ocean than to take from your soul the faith in its mission.

You have been appointed among My sisters and brothers because it is just that we should meet again after your long seeking after the Master who introduced you to the Truth and the Way to immortal life. I want to impress upon you today the integration of your selves and efforts on the divine plane for the fulfilment of your individual divine entities. From now on, cast aside as useless and dangerous every thought and refrain from every act that does not fit in with that divinely ordained plan. Verily, verily, I say unto you, you will soon be able to enter voluntarily the Kingdom of Eternal Life and see the pattern of things to come. Prepare for that great moment when you will recognise My face and My presence. All that is from the lower world does not belong to you, My sisters. The only bond should be your desire to accomplish your mission.

Kneel and say the Prayer of the Blessing so that My Spirit can descend unto you. I bless you with the peace and serenity that will carry you through the ordeals at hand. You shall soon hear My voice again, and feel My presence near your closed eyes, opened to eternal beauties.

❧❀☙

November 15th, 1944
from St. Francis — through Ninon

The Voice of the Silence can only be heard when all noises of worldly turmoil have stopped. If you try to hear it in the midst of worldly turmoil, deafness will stop your ears, still unprepared for the blessed melody. The soul must listen again to its Maker before trying anew to catch what can only be heard by those in whom every faculty is tuned harmoniously for the supreme test. You are both very much nearer than you think to the goal towards which you are striving through your united efforts. Smile, my dearest ones, smile, and let my blessing pour on you and on this house where your friends from the other world will speak to you. Concerning the Holy Cup you will receive instructions from the Master himself. We are well pleased with you. Say your prayer with ringing conviction. I will preside over your holy meditation and draw the blue force over your tender bodies and your strong souls. Receive my love, Francis

❧❀☙

November 21st, 1944

The Holy Mountain [a state of being] is nearer than you think and already your faltering steps are headed its way. Be glad, My daughters, and bear that gladness in your hearts as My undying present because you have been blessed by the touch of the Divine Love that pours from the Father through Me. Do not be afraid, sisters, as you have been chosen; even if the way is arduous the reward will be so glorious that you will wonder at your dismay. Remember that no joy can be fulfilled and breathed in unless one has been prepared by a price of sorrowful experience in the eyes of those who do not know, but those who know — those who have been elected to see through the mysteries of everlasting life — know that there is no sorrow nor pain, no more than there is death, because these are only the negative side of joy, of gladness, just as there is no beauty without its contrary, ugliness, and there could be no resurrection without the passage through the grave.

That is what I tried to teach humanity through My way to the cross which is no symbol of sorrow but of the greatest blessing on earth — that of understanding crossed with love. This state I tried to teach to My inner core of disciples before I took leave of them on the sacred Mount. This is a symbol that you will learn to know and to master and to use as you now learn to know to master and to use the symbol of the Cup. But for that you need to have passed through the third Gateway which will be at the time when the New Age will be heralded, as the liquidation of the old one will have taken place. You will have to wait some time as only the Father knows of the exact moment when this will take place. First the balance between good and evil must be weighed so that the Law be fulfilled and evolution be resumed as it was written in the Books of Wisdom of past ages. I dearly love you My daughters, and depart from you from for some hours. In the name of the Father, I extend My blessing on you.

❧❀☙

November 22nd, 1944
Thalia, Ninon and Lilla — through Ninon

The peace of the Spirit be on you three, My treasured circle. Well have you passed the day, and with great clairvoyance did your intuition lead you by the hand in all your steps, even those that seemed merely worldly. Truly did you cling to the true rope which is the hope and the salvation of this world today. You shall go now into the Hall of Learning to discover the hidden meaning of the symbols which are but the shadows of burning, flaming truths. The meaning also of what you call the Grail. The mystery of the Holy Cup shall be revealed to you in time.

You can use the blessing of the Father, the Son, and the Holy Spirit on yourselves tonight after having formed your group with the urgent and compassionate desire to help your neighbour as you help yourself. This is the first step in the development of your future mission and I say unto you now with ringing voice, "In the name of the Father — the head, the Son — the heart, and the Holy Spirit, I extend My blessing hand on you."

$$\mathscr{RC} \oplus \mathscr{RS}$$

December 3rd, 1944
Thalia and Ninon — through Ninon

Peace be on you, My beloved daughters. I am speaking without restraint to you at this hour as you have been so well prepared. I am well satisfied with you, My faithful disciples. Later this evening My friend and devoted messenger Francis who is by My side now, will tell you why you have deserved to progress a step more on the way to the Holy Mountain. Verily, verily, I say unto you, peace be on your brow, peace be in your heart. Let the Spirit of Peace, which is the true servant of the Father, be with you everlastingly.

Into My Temple did you penetrate this evening and what did you see? Did you see faith? True devotion? No, you saw only the images of the Truth, the Truth that was in your heart that instant. You were chosen when the time came, you and all the other groups which are being prepared under My guidance or the guidance of one of My brothers to re-establish the truth of the Father, the true Word that was Mine, and to help with the purification of religion which is to come with the great upheaval.

Man has been thrown prey to the forces of matter in order to realise that the way to truth and life can only come through inner understanding, faith, and love. When the elements of matter will rise up against the sinning man and strike him, he will cry out, "Woe is me! What have I done? I have chosen power and domination instead of faith and love?" And he will seek the way to the Mountain to save himself from the Catastrophe, but only those who have chosen Faith when the rest of the world was still blinded can go the way to the mountain of salvation. The others will have to die and be born again with the desire of the true Law in their hearts before they too can go the Way that you are going.

You will need all the strength of the prayer that you are learning gradually to master, to go the hard, uplifting way of the mountain. In the Church with you were thousands of My messengers trying to speak to deaf ears My message of love, and the prayer that goes to the Father and brings back the Holy Spirit. Did you hear the music of their wings? Try to lift up your vibrations after your prayer and you may hear that celestial harmony. Do not reject the cup of bitterness that will be extended to you on the Way. Through prayer, mastered through self-discipline and used for the sake of all those who are now on this planet — the true sons of God — be they My followers or those of My Brothers, the bitterness can be changed to sweetness more inspiring than the sweetness which springs from its antithesis. Such is the miracle of the Transfiguration. In it lies the meaning of the Grail, the mystic cup of suffering which blossoms to those and for those who can see beyond the mysteries of matter. You too, will see it, My daughters, when you are ready. Today I have told you enough of its true Nature for you to meditate upon and to see the first beams of the purifying light.

Pray, pray, and be incessantly ready, expectant, and faithful, because only prayer and faith will lead you the Way that I go before you, as I did before. Never forget your spiritual encounter in the middle of the day. Verily I say unto you, it would be better for you to lose one of your eyes than to miss the mystic strength ever reinforced by your meetings under My guidance on the astral plane. Drink the cup of purity with Me as did My first followers. Drink it deeply as you pray. Make from your prayer in the frame of the Holy Cup, an armour so strong that it can never be shaken. Pray, pray, and watch. You will see the Holy Cup. In the name of the Father, the Son, and the Holy Spirit.

❧ ✿ ☙

January 1st, 1945
Thalia and Ninon — through Ninon

Peace to be on you, my daughters. Yes, I am among you, your Lord and your Master. My hand presses to your lips the Holy Cup of Everlasting Life, with its dregs of bitterness and of sorrow, but with the strength and the perfume of God in its iridescent drops.

You have served Me well in this past year and have gone your way with steadfast Faith. Verily, verily, I say unto you, do not mind the temptations and the seeds of the past, but look up at the stars and wait for the vision that will entrance your sight and make your spirit tremble with a shaking joy, like the joy of the child who sees the milk of his mother. O children of mine, whom I bless with My Love, verily have you been like the wise Virgins and treasured the oil of wisdom that has been given unto you.

It was My wish that you should celebrate together the festival of My birth since this birth has more meaning this year than in any other year, because the times are near when My words, which were given unto Me by the Father, must be fulfilled. The cycle is completed. As in the past, My disciples are gathering in My name, their hearts glowing with purity and with the light of heaven on their faces. They have chased away the fear — their and My worst enemy — and they do not dread the world anymore because the world has surrendered to their faith in the Father. Persecutions may come, not on the material but on the spiritual plane, and the enemies of God may laugh at you and try to drown you in the ocean of their own despair. But they will fail. This time My word will come true and I will fulfil My covenant with those who believed in Me when I trod the sands of Palestine.

Verily, verily, I say unto you, great will be the work you will have to do in My name. And do not say, "Lord, I am not ready!" You will be ready when the time comes because you will lend your frail bodies to My strength. Do not complain, "Lord, my feeble mind cannot grasp your mysteries!" These mysteries which are of the Father are not for the human mind to grasp as it can grasp an article in the paper or a political discussion. They are revealed to the understanding by the Radiant Ones who stand at their sides, bit by bit, because if taken all at once, it would destroy their individual minds, as it is only safely perceptible with the Divine Wisdom of the Everlasting One.

But did you forget that I promised to those who knocked, that the door would be opened unto them? If the door opened straight away and you could see into the eternity of the future, it is probable that you would stumble and hurt yourselves. But keep knocking, children of My Living Word, and gently, very gently will the door open so that you will have time to prepare and bear the radiance of the vision that will fill your mind with the realisation of the immortal truth. Two thousand years have I waited! Should you get impatient and wail, "When will the day come? When will I be fully prepared?" Each day, each minute, you are being prepared, and the truth comes nearer and nearer to you as does the Holy Mountain.

This year, My beloved ones, is to be full of strange, mysterious happenings. Discontent and trouble will spread among the rulers of the earth and the enemy will take the cloak of the lamb. Each time those who go the way of the world will believe that their hour of triumph has come. Each time it will be denied, because the only possible triumph is My triumph and not theirs. And so, daughters, do not rejoice hastily, but neither despair hastily, because it will always be the unexpected that will happen and not that for which people, including you, have prepared in the worldly way.

The time has come for My disciples to gather so that the frightened and the worldly, but who still have a soul to save, may be encouraged so that, when the time comes, they may go to them and ask for the truth. Re-read the chronicles about the early spread of My Faith, and those concerning the Holy Cup. Much of what you need to know lies in their midst for you to discover. And with your new awareness, you will discover it quickly and well.

And now, I bless you, and I extend My hands over your brow. Meet again tomorrow to meditate on the message you have been given. There is no more appropriate beginning of the year for you. I will come in your midst when you say again your prayer of devotion, and enshroud you in the blue light of Love. My prayer of invocation should be said by you every morning. Go in peace and pray in My name. Blessings, blessings on you, My beloved daughters.

❧ ✿ ☙

January 20, 1945
Thalia and Ninon, from St. Francis — through Ninon

Greetings, dear children of the light. I, Francis, have come to speak with you about the new teachings that you have been so privileged to receive. I am glad that you are making notes that will help you to acquire a clear knowledge of the facts that are gradually being given to you. You are, as you have been told many times, under trial. Opportunities are offered to you that of your own free will must be taken full advantage of, if you would pass the tests and measure up to the standard expected of you. You are sometimes slow in appreciating this, but so far you have, in your own time, come to the realisation of what is expected of you. Let us see a stepping up your pace from now on. Fear not that this might cause you to lose your balance, for this is as firm as the bedrock. It is the energetic application of your minds to facts that are now being given to you that you may later give out as solid facts to others. Could anything be more conducive to giving you the necessary balance you need to go through the cataclysm? In contrast, the worst preparation you could possibly accord yourselves is drifting along in an aimless and hopeless sort of way like a ship without anchor or rudder.

I will leave you now with this message and my love. I will come again tomorrow night with a longer message to you.

❧ ✿ ☙

January 21st, 1945
Thalia and Ninon — through Ninon from St. Francis

O darling children, my most beloved daughters, it is indeed your Francis, coming to you this evening with a quite special message of love and understanding. I have been with you for quite a while directing your meetings and guiding your thoughts. The dear Master, the Beloved One, asked me first to extend His blessings on you. He will speak to you again in Washington. He is very busy, as the time is so short and so many need His help and His encouragement. But He is always very near you as He has chosen you and you have rejoiced His heart by your faithfulness and your selfless attachment to His service. Indeed, what He has in store for you is great and inspiring. Such pure joy will be yours and such entire gladness will be in your hearts when you attain the top of the Holy Mountain where you are due! I may say to you tonight in great discretion and confidence but from it you will discover the New Jerusalem and you will be given the mission that is going to fulfil your wishes of ages, indeed since the beginning of this Cycle.

You will suddenly understand the reasons for all your pains, sufferings and trials. They will seem to you so insignificant, so small in comparison to what you have attained, that you will wonder that at one time you could have been filled with them and have judged your life by such fleeting values. May I explain, dearest ones? It is just as the patient who must undergo an operation to save his very life. Even if he is told that the operation is safe and his doctor a wonderful man, the thought of it and the fear of it may overshadow his mind and he may forget that his life is going to be saved through it. But after he wakes up from his narcotic sleep, he suddenly realises that the operation is over, that he is saved, and that in a few days he will be healthy and strong as he was not before. Such is often the interpretation that a mind should give to pain and sufferings. These are just the blessed trials that will in the course of time save your life and bring you to your real state, which for your body is health and harmony, for the soul immortality and liberation from karma. I hope you will meditate on these words as they are very important for you at this time.

I am the Soul of Love and one of the forerunners of the New Age. Of that Age I must speak — I must sing — for it is too beautiful for words. You need the voices of the Archangels and the Heavenly Choir to describe it properly. It will be like the dew of the morning touched by the gold of the sun, with the perfume of all the roses in the world and delicate harmonies to enshrine it. It will be like the song of birds as they fly in the most beautiful evening sky, the dazzling glimmer of the stars on their feathers. It will be like the moon bursting into thousands of particles, like harps with the caress of many winds whispering over them. Oh, it will be so beautiful when the Kingdom is established that no one still on this plane can realise it without feeling dazed. The Son of Man will come and so gentle will be His words for His faithful servants that no human imagination, nor even that of the angels, can ever conceive of such gentleness, for his wrath is not for you and you will gladly have endured the wrath of the entire world to be spared even one of His words of righteous anger. Your longing will be satisfied and your only desire will be to help with us those who still need a loving hand to stumble upward along the long road of evolution until another chance is offered to them to take the shortcut.

This should encourage you, my blessed children, for indeed if you follow carefully the teaching given unto you, you will see Him, the Mighty One, and the beloved Beings at Whose feet you will find immortality and eternal peace, not only for you but for those you will be allowed to save. Love be with you, in Radiance and in Faith await the coming of the Rider on the White Horse, the Lord of Liberation. I bless you again in my name and in the name of the Master.

❦

February 10th, 1945
Thalia and Ninon — through Ninon

Blessings, My dearest children, blessings. Great and strong are the Forces of Light spreading out from My hands to the world like great golden arrows that pierce the hearts of the unbelievers and upset their minds. To those who are awakened, they reveal the sources of light and of understanding. This is the secret meaning the stigmata — another of My symbols that you will have to grasp in time. I want to teach you today some necessary truths if you are to serve Me well.

Yes, it is My desire and the will of the Father that you become the servants of the New Age, the true priests of Him who will reveal to the world the marvels of the Kingdom of Heaven. Of this Kingdom, My brother, Francis, spoke to you when he described to you, its beauty. But, daughters of My spoken word, you have still to learn and to unfold before you can realise this mission. Verily, verily, I say unto you, you shall only see the Kingdom of Heaven and the glory of the Son of Man if you steel your will and reinforce your gift of spiritual vision. Truly I am well satisfied with your devotion and your faith, but you still lack the strength and power to fulfil your great task. When you are united and together, you are strengthened and inspired and all is as it should be. When you are separated, you often, without knowing it, fall back from the high standards I have set for you and relax in beatitude and what you, in perfect good faith, call spiritual meditation. But My daughters, hear and hearken to My words, the time is too short for that kind of beatitude. It will be yours after the law of the Father has come to pass and My mission has been fulfilled.

You must prepare for action and hard action, as the way you have to follow is uphill and rocky. You must develop your other centres as well as the love-heart centre. You need the power to act. You need a strong will to go through the upheavals ahead of you and humanity, or you will not be able to go through. You will sink into impersonal bliss and lose your individuality. This is not My wish and you would disappoint Me if you should follow that way.

I love you dearly, as I told you before, because of old ties and because there is a definite place for you in the Plan of the things that will come to pass even if they seem to you to be delayed. You must do everything in your power to increase your knowledge. Manage your emotions and strengthen your minds. When your mind is strengthened, then the force of your love, which is your devotion, will flow back to you and others with added quality. This quality will enable you to go much farther and faster on the Way we wish you to go.

Yes, you are meant to serve on the Blue Ray (Love-Wisdom), but as a good student only specialises when he has gone through a general course of studies to keep his knowledge well balanced, so must My pupils specialise only when their knowledge of all the ways is great enough to enable them to say "I know", when they will be called upon to teach. But now I must prepare you for what will come to pass, and that is why you must avoid — not complacency, I never meant this — but relaxation. You are on the Path and you have to go quickly if you want to be in time to welcome the Son of Man and see Me. Verily, verily, I say unto you, dearest ones, you have to prepare for the fateful ringing of the bells, and be strong enough to overcome the bewilderment that will follow it. And you will need every bit of the strength that you still have to overcome the depression that will fall on you then. Far better to be a little disturbed now by the friendly touch of a loving hand than to be overthrown by the terrible wind that will then shake the world.

The Holy Cup will appear symbolically in heaven at the end of this Age and will stand over the head of the Son of Man. The chosen ones and you will see Me overshadowed by the God of the Blue Light, as big as one side of heaven, extending My hands in benediction over the whole regenerate earth with the cross of light and life, the new symbol which is destined to replace the cross of sorrow. For truly with the coming of the Son of Man, the Rider on the White Horse, will the evil be conquered. Matter will be raised to spirit, and no more spirit lowered into matter. Meditate. I bless you. I will send Francis to explain what you still find difficult to understand. I send My golden arrows to your forehead, your heart, and your throat. Your Master.

❧ ❀ ☙

February 11th, 1945
Thalia and Ninon — through Ninon

Good morning, dear children of light. As promised, I have come back, always devoted to the enlightenment of your minds and souls. I am the messenger of love, as I told you, and I speak to you on a point of red-golden light with a halo of blue light surrounding me and you.

I have something of importance to say: I want to tell you, dearest ones, that the wrong idea of the suffering of the great being — Christ — was the terrible mistake that gave rise to the dreadful karma of Nazism. Nazism was the direct consequence of that grievous error which glorified physical suffering instead of seeing its symbolical meaning.

The wine shown by Master Jesus, inspired by Christ, at the Last Supper to His disciples, was the fruit of the vine, because blood was meant to be understood symbolically by the Master, never literally. The vibration of human blood is of a very low order if not spiritualised by the orange force of Nature. That is why the Master used wine, dipped and magnetised in the orange force of Nature, and not blood.

When [as Joseph of Arimathea] I was told to take the cup of the Last Supper and go to receive a few drops of the blood of the Master, I did not understand at first what was meant by this act. When the blood was dried by the radiant golden light of the sun — not the same day — but the day after, when the Master had already risen, I suddenly got the divine illumination and realised that the suffering and agony of the body were being overcome by the power from above, and that truly the transubstantiation had taken place. This miracle was to be forever glorified and remain as an example for generations to come. [5]

What did the lower minds of men make of this Divine Truth? Led astray by the lower vibration of the dark red force, they suggested to humanity to worship not the divine, sun-raised fruit of the vine, but human blood, in the contemplation of the suffering of the Divine Spirit. They truly crucified it again and again in their blind misunderstanding of the Divine Wisdom. They placed the focus of their worship on the crucifixion, and the sacrificial death, rather than on the resurrection. The evil spirit of Judas, who is on the dark red current and is the enemy of Christ as the expression of the blue force of love, revenged itself on humanity by spreading this ghastly error. [6]

In my mission as St. Francis, I tried to put humanity right on this matter by teaching the love of Nature and by trying to brighten the spirit of religion at that time. I did not succeed, as the Church was already condemned by its greed and its spiritual blindness. It was the last chance given to the Roman Church. Now, in our times, the cult of blood has flourished in the black magic in which Nazism is steeped. Their worship of blood and race, without the remembrance of God to throw a ray of hope on this ghastly error, has drawn upon the world, which did not protest and seek knowledge, the awful bloodbath which has been going on since the First World War started.

Now I have given you these explanations so that you may see how important it is that you clarify all your mental images on these fundamental matters. The least bit of hesitancy or confusion on your part may have terrible consequences for you and others. We wish you to avoid them, as we think you have so much to give through the love-centre you have created.

5. In the Christian tradition the Eucharist is the most important ritual in the church. The bread or 'wafer' that the celebrants are given to eat represents Jesus' body and the wine, sipped from a chalice, his blood. The emphasis being on the pain, suffering and sacrifice that he endured rather than the miracle of life after death – the Resurrection.

6. Compare the words of these two Gospels to see where the emphasis ought to have been. Firstly, the Gospel of John 6:53-54. Then Jesus said unto them, "Verily, verily, I say unto you, except ye eat of the flesh of the Son of Man, and drink his blood, ye have no life in you. Whoso eateth my flesh and drinketh my blood, hath eternal life; and I will raise him up at the last day."

    and The Gospel of the Beloved Companion 18:8, page 36. And Yeshua said to them, "Only from the truth I tell you, unless you eat of the very flesh of the Son of Humanity, which is his teachings, and drink of his very blood, which is his words, you will not have life in yourselves. Whosoever eats of my teachings and drinks my words, has eternal life and will never die."

❀

February 26th, 1945
New York — Thalia, Ninon and others — through Ninon

Blessings, dearest children. How glad we are to find you all gathered in our name. I come with the message from the Master, but I am a newcomer in your midst. I waited for an opportunity to come through to you to help you to carry out the Master's work. My name is of no importance for the time being but you all knew me at the same place and at the same moment of your evolution. I am as quick as fire, and I can do much to help you in your evolutionary struggle.

The time has come when you can talk freely of the time you spent together in Palestine, who you were, and how you served Him who is inspiring you. Your common bond was at that time and what you have to do now is to concentrate on what you were supposed to do then but could not accomplish. You were all among the Holy Women who helped to spread the first teachings of Christianity. Christianity took the wrong path, and it is your common karma, now, at the end of the Age to help put the error straight, to make Light where there was shadow, to implant faith where doubt was lurking. This is a terrific responsibility and it is because the Master feels how tremendous your task is that he has put so much time and care into your preparation.

Each of you has to take a certain angle of Faith and Religion and strengthen knowledge on this matter and wait for further guidance and inspiration. Naturally, you have to expect tremendous trials, as the enemies of God and humanity do not see with pleasure such progress being made, as it means their ultimate downfall. You are meant to meditate on these important matters of Faith and Religion and find out where you went wrong in your first teachings so as not to make the same mistake again. Your creed must be simple and suited to the ignorant as well as to the wise. The World Teacher is directing His will towards you and asking you, the pupils and friends and relations of His Beloved Son, to take seriously your responsibilities. The need is great and the time is short. My brother Francis will give you soon a short message which will guide you a little more in the technique of your preparation. Now I will answer one or two questions if that is your wish. Your devoted servant...[no name]

Answer to a question:

You have been brought together to share the responsibility that was yours in ancient times. The Holy Women played a great part in the early spreading of the Faith. Re-read what happened at the time of Constantine [7] and it will enlighten you. You have all the same duty today, to prepare and to do better this time.

7. The Council of Nicaea AD 325, when the Doctrine of the Trinity was created and Jesus was declared to be the only Son of God, of the same substance as God. It was the time of the persecution of the Gnostics and the destruction of the Gnostic texts that miraculously surfaced in 1945 at Nag Hammadi, in Egypt.

An additional message from St. Francis:

Good evening, my dear ones. I do not want you to go until I have given you my fond greeting as a group, that will henceforth work closely together. And in the new strength that this cohesion will give you, you will accomplish your great mission. Long, long has it been necessary to wait until the cycle should bring you back to that place where you could pick up the threads of your destinies and your mission and complete it in the way you did not succeed in doing in that earlier time. Because you failed then, the task of succeeding now has become greater and more difficult but also the triumph will be greater because, on this higher turn of the spiral, more can be accomplished as more people are ready to receive the Light and humanity as a whole, is a step nearer the goal. My love goes with you as you disperse for a time. Francis

February 27th, 1945
Thalia, Ninon and Lilla — through Ninon

My fondest greetings, dearest ones. Yes, I have been with you the whole evening, listening to your conversation and directing the trend of your thoughts. Open and receptive did I find your minds and my heart was gladdened by such conditions. I wanted so much to get through to you tonight of all nights. So much of what I have to say will help and enlighten you.

In answer to your question, I think that already we have tried to make clear to all of you that indeed there could be no question of pity or sentimentality in the form of fulfilment of your task. You can offer those people you would like to save with the opportunities of redeeming themselves. Just now, there are many apparently old and inveterate sinners who, in the depths of their disregarded soul and higher selves, are beginning to hear a small voice telling them that they have erred in their ways. These sinners may be saved even at the last minute, nay at the last second. That is why no one should be thought unworthy until he has definitely refused the saving hand. Your attitude — as this is meant for the three of you — must be one of firm dignity and simple kindliness. Do not rush after people; wait for them. If the voice of their higher nature is heard in time, they will come to you and catch your outstretched, helping hand. What you are not allowed or supposed to do is to force your hand under their unwilling arm and drag them uphill with you. That would be wrong and working against the Law. The only and sure result would be that you would stumble and falter, and while you are spending precious time and energy helping the unworthy, you would not be available for those who you are really meant to help.

Bear well in mind, as this is important, that the best you can do for others depends on the best you can do for yourselves — I mean for your Higher Mind. If you have really conquered all your unworthy impulses, this fact in itself must be of tremendous help to others and encourage them to follow the same way, which is the only way of real salvation. Many, many people nowadays who are weak, not evil, are led astray for lack of examples which they could follow fearlessly as a proof of the ways taken by Eternal Truth to manifest itself. Who can really believe in an astute priest, or a politically good man, or in those who may follow the letter of religion but never the spirit? Words have lost so much of their meaning that only actions can redeem them.

You must ACT your belief, dearest children, and live according to your faith, and the rest will be easy. It is not necessary for you to go on the roof and shout your creed at the top of your voice, straining your lungs and injuring your vocal cords. There must be a light in your eyes, a poise in your being, a warmth in your smile that speak more loudly to those who want to hear all the words you have not spoken but have lived out. That is enough, more than enough to break down the defences of those who are only bewildered and who prefer to follow tradition rather than real thought. It will get your message through to those who have a spark in them to be awakened. Go your way, daughters of mine, calm, poised, and serene, and you will be true helpers and not nervous and distressed would-be kind souls who are of service to nobody, including their own higher nature. This was the message I had to deliver tonight. If you have more questions, sleep on them and I will answer you tomorrow during your meditation.

Your loving Francis, who hovers over your auras.

❧ ❀ ☙

February 28th, 1945
Thalia, Ninon and Lilla — through Ninon

Good morning, children. I am here with you as you rightly detected. I see with pleasure that you have perfectly understood my message yesterday. I must indeed impress you once more with the earnestness of your responsibility. Remember that you become as a mother and father to those you want to save and that you can only care for some elected few. Kindness is a very notable quality, so is sympathy; emotion and sentimentality are not.

I see the question in Ninon's mind, and I must answer: you are right, my child, it was indeed emotion that was your mistake at the beginning of this Cycle. Emotion is dangerous because it can so easily become its very antithesis, and selfishness become egoism; pity, self-indulgence. The emotional display of Faith has too easily replaced the serene knowledge of perfect understanding. That is why I urge you to increase your mental power and to develop your knowledge. You can only teach what you know and understand or you can easily become dogmatic and block the creative drive in those you have to awaken.

The New Age has to be serene on the mental plane or it cannot be. You see how important it is to put your knowledge so precisely and so clearly that you can impress the minds without having to stir the dregs of emotional devotion. Devotion is not Faith and this time we want faith and knowledge, not devotion and emotion. This does not mean that we want you cold-blooded. Around All and in All runs the Divine Power of Love, but that Love must come from its higher centres and not the lower ones so that it can reach the Higher Realms of Divine Life. I hope this will help you to face your task. As you know already, only those who can acquire these qualities will be able to pass through into the New Age as our servants and beloved daughters. My love, Francis

❧❀☙

March 18th, 1945
Thalia, Ninon and Lilla — through Ninon

Greetings, and showers of blessings on my dear, dear children of Light. I am here with you as you read again the past words of revelation and glean from them new facets of truth that they hold for you. Thalia shall take out from the pages [of the Messages] significant passages for her sisters. Lilla shall do the same from such pages as she has in her keeping. And Ninon shall contribute from out of her intuition. Thus, shall be built up a true rendering of great and important truths and revelation. I shall answer some of the points that you have questioned tomorrow morning. Now I want to tell you that your work must go on no matter what the outer conditions of your lives in the days that are before you — that is, it must be carried on as uninterruptedly as possible. Ninon will be able to go into the public library and books will be put into her hands to answer your questions and fill in the gaps as well as confirm what you have already learnt.

Because of the serious way that you have undertaken your pursuit of truth and knowledge, you have set in motion forces that will play into your hands and will guide you to the object of your search. Having set this in motion, you do not want to let drop your work so well begun simply because outer events press on you for attention. See that at least part of each day is faithfully given to this most important work. And now my dearest ones, I see that the Master is ready with His message for you and I will step aside for the moment. Francis

While Ninon was writing the last sentence, they heard a loud knocking…

Peace be to you, My daughters, peace be to you. Yes, it was I that you heard loudly knocking at the door of your hearts united in love and in service. I stand before you as I stood before My disciples as they discussed My resurrection and saw Me in their midst. What they did not relate, because it was too secret, is that in My hands I held again the Cup of Life as I had held it at the Last Supper. This Cup of Light burned before their eyes with the flame of the jewel of Love. But the world was not ready, only the chosen ones. I did not fail in My mission, but I had to wait for the further evolution of humanity; for the time was not ripe for the seeds that were prepared for that time to be gathered by the four winds of heaven and flung back where they belong, on the face of the earth, making it blossom in its richest harvest since the beginning of the ages. No, the time was not ripe, so the seeds were buried in the bowels of the earth and hidden in the hearts of My disciples until the time should come when the Word of the Father could be fulfilled.

I asked you to study the first development of My Faith, and rightly were you told that it spread through little groups of people who gathered in My name, and to these little groups was the truth revealed in the true meaning of My teachings and the lessons I had brought to the world through the divine inspiration that was given unto Me by the Father, the Red Angel.

But the lower spirit of man, roused by ambition and greed, fallaciously penetrated My teaching, and incorporated it to the cause of Caesar. And I had said, "Render unto Caesar the things which are Caesar's, and unto God the things that are God's." But Caesar took My word and made it into his own. While My true followers had to flee, pursued by the double scourge of Judas and Caesar, the truth burnt out and the stone of mystery was hidden in the bowels of the earth. It was not hidden in one place only; no, I had given instructions to him who was My most trusted follower, as I had seen his spirit wreathed in the agony of his humility. I had given him who was Joseph — who later was Francis — the secret into his safe-keeping.

Two stones there were: on one was to be built the visible house, and this was given to Peter. The one that would help My invisible house to be built when the times were ripe for the enlightenment of all those were worthy of their humanity, and for whom only the Son of Man was to bring forth the mysteries of the Son of God, this stone I entrusted to Francis, My well-beloved. Well-nigh did he build on it the true House of God, but he too did not succeed as the times were not ripe.

As the one who sat at the head of the table, I tried again to draw the attention of erring humanity to the secrets of the Cup that was a rose and a stone [the Grail], but only the purest of the pure could see the true mysteries hidden behind the legend, and then in collective misinterpretation did they go to the Holy Land to seek what was not there to find. It had gone West with the little group of My faithful disciples. Francis knew, but he too had to wait as the time had not yet come. The stone was hidden and the seat was empty.

When another chance was given humanity to reform and to listen to My voice, the ones who are appointed to speak in My name failed Me and did not accept the price of love and the cross of My life, but chose to follow their own way and to speak in their own name and not in mine [Reformation]. Thus, from folly to folly and misinterpretation did humanity come to the End of the Age when the scores have to be settled.

Hark to My words, daughters of the Living Word, yours is the task to serve and to teach, and to open the secrets that lie buried in the hearts of the chosen ones. Do not be apprehensive. You will be given the strength and the knowledge necessary by the Holy Spirit that speaks through the throat centre, having penetrated your heads through its finest centres. When the touch of the divine fire will be on you, then will your memories be so strengthened that you will remember all that is necessary for you to remember of the past and the Word of God will pass easily through you as the wind that blows in the morning through the grass. Your perfect unity is already a symbol of the New Age. You are being prepared to vibrate like the harp of the Lord, and mighty, burning truths will come through your lips and you will remember, remember, remember.

The sign will come from the East, and the fire of heaven will reveal the Truth from the bowels of the Earth. Suddenly, you will stand up like arrows of faith and from the top of the Holy Mountain start on your common mission of building My New House where the Lord of Liberation will dwell. Each of you will preach in her own way that particular aspect of the Word that will be given unto her to reveal. And then you will meet the Mighty One, and behind Him you will see My arms extended in benediction. No longer will I be called the Man of Sorrows but the Man of Joy, as My task will be fulfilled. I can gladly come forward after the Rider shall have passed this way and made his harvest of good souls, and announced the glad tidings of the Coming of the Divine One, in whom the Love of God is all and universal. You will see all of this happen, My servants faithful and loving, if you stay like the wise virgins, well-prepared and ever obedient.

This will be after the Bells have rung and the water and the fire will have cleansed the world. Now, may My peace and My love penetrate your souls and raise them to the first gleams of the Light that was in the Cup and which now lies buried, biding the time of revelation. You will be entrusted with this Holy Flame, O red roses of service, My devoted ones, who will no more disobey.

❧ ✦ ☙

March 19th, 1945
Thalia, Ninon and Lilla — through Ninon

Good morning again, dearest ones. I was with you while you re-read your message from last night and I can tell you that on the whole, your intuition guided you to the right answers. Naturally, there are still some deep esoteric truths that you can only partially understand, in their full implications. The Master bids me to tell you that if you keep your mind turned to their solution, progressively you will discover more and more meaning to what has just been told to your group. The esoteric meaning must be discovered by you gradually through concentrated exercise of your power of thought, that will bring back from the treasures of the past, memories that are necessary for you to grasp fully what is necessary in the present.

On three periods should you concentrate your reading: the early spread of Christianity; the First Crusade; and the time of the Reformation. You know enough for the moment on Arthur's time and on my time as St. Francis. Let Ninon study the early spread of the Faith, Lilla the First Crusade and Thalia the Reformation through her contact with Charles V. That man was an initiate and had conceived a great task. Isabella [of Portugal] was placed at his side to help him accomplish this task with her wonderful insight into the higher realities. But Charles failed a test that had to be put to him because of old karma, so Isabella was taken from him because she would have suffered too much to see her dream crushed. Philip, his son, who was attracted to him because of this same karma, distorted his father's great idea and, together with Luther and Judas, who was reincarnated at that time, represented the terrible triangle of distorted purpose, through the use of a strong Faith without the Light of God, so that the Faith became

Fire and the Fire scourged the world that was meant for love and joy.

These fires are burning still. They have served, as did the wrong interpretation of the crucifixion of our Lord, the cause of the enemy of man, fighting to prevent the coming of the Son of Man, that we may also call the Fulfiller. **Only when men learn not to shed their brother's blood in cruel wars, can the house of God be built on its true foundations**. Until this moment comes shall Caesar, as the Master said, unjustly usurp the power that is God's, because those who ought to have chosen God chose Caesar and you see the results today. We must be clear and confess that all of us, if only for a few seconds of our eternity, were responsible for this state of things. Even I had to expiate my false vanity and caution. That is why we had to suffer so much to repair the evil that we had sown throughout our foolishness.

Caesar's spirit came into the first Church and sat enthroned in Rome, and the Church fought with the arms of man instead of fighting with the arms of God which are prayer: only prayer, meditation, and concentration in the service of the Divine Plan. Now, my dearest daughters, that you know the will of the Master and at least the trend of the Divine Plan, if not its actual contents, be humbler and more loving than ever. Your prayer is to God expressing Himself to you through both Christ and the Master Jesus. When it speaks of the One who is all, it speaks of God. The Guide is your Master, and the love goes to Christ. This is the perfect triangle to which all perfect triangles should pray, as this is the time of the Second Coming. I bless you in Divine Love, Francis

❧ ❀ ☙

May 20th, 1945
Pentecost — Thalia, Lilla and Ninon — through Ninon

The Light be on you, daughters of the Burning Truth. The Light be on your brow, the Light be on your heart, The Light be on your throat, so that you may be purified and become the welcome channels of the Word of God. Meditate on this most awe-inspiring responsibility of yours. If you are pure like the flame or the blade of the Higher One, you have nothing to fear, but verily, verily, I say unto you, My well-beloved ones, if you should not be as pure as the morning dew, then indeed will the flame of the Word burn you and you would be consumed in the sense of your unfulfilled mission. But you have been prepared and I know you will not fail Me. But I have to make you realise that thin is the divide between fulfilment and failure; accomplishment, and sinking into the depths of unbelieving despair.

Today, on the celebration of the descent of the Spirit of Truth into the hearts of men, I want to have you look steadily into the times to come and say loudly and with ringing voice, "I accept the responsibility of spreading the Word of God because I know that never before has it been needed so much by My bewildered brothers and sisters of the human race!" I had warned you and prepared you for the ringing of the bells. The bells have rung and peace has not come to this erring Earth; on the contrary, peace has been pushed back from it, and on the plane close to this Earth, gloating forces are waiting for their evil opportunity.

Salvation can yet be gained if the Word be spread today, My daughters. I declare to you, verily, verily, it is time for My warriors to be ready for their Crusade for Truth, Love, and Wisdom. The Vigil of Purity is being held. I appoint you the disciples of the New Age. The time has come; I will teach personally your enlarged group. From now on you are in active service. You will only lay down your arms of Peace when the Lord of Liberation will descend to crown your efforts. Onwards, faithful and devoted ones! The time has come. I bless you and extend My hands on your brow so that the way for Truth be opened; over your heart, so that you be consumed by your Love for My Service; over your throat, so that you could bring the Word home to your brethren. Peace be your vocation under the glorious banner of your way to My Cross of Light.

May 21st, 1945
Thalia and Ninon — through Ninon

Good morning, dearest sisters, good morning. I am here and well pleased with your serene acceptance of your future task. Truly you have deserved to be among the disciples of the beloved Master as you have answered His call with gladness and joy; the call that you had waited for all through the dark ages. It came as the true ringing of the bells of eternal life, the only one that truly announces the return of Heavenly Peace on this shattered world. I have not much more to say, only that in the days to come you have work with all these new disciples who will have been gathered by the Will of the Lord so that you may be ready to face the task confronting you as the day approaches. Meet as often as you can. My love will always hover over your heads as the Dove of the Messenger. Your devoted friend and brother, Francis

❦❀❧

Pentecost 1945 — The Crescent Moon
Thalia and Ninon

This is Asraf speaking, your devoted friend between heaven and earth. Just a few words to explain to you the meaning of the Crescent Moon. It is one of the most important signs of the zodiac. If fulfilment comes with the full of the moon, it is under the Crescent that all inventions or innovations start.

> It is the sign of renewal.
> It is the sign of the Eternal Feminine aspect
>   of all things in the cosmos.
> It is a sign of the arts and intuition.

All the daughters of the Crescent Moon have in common a very strong intuitive feminine quality in their souls. They love art and further the course of art. Science hurts their sensitivity. They are mostly happy in the company of flowers and affectionate, amiable companions. The rose is the natural companion to the Crescent Moon, and also certain herbs that live in southern countries.

It is a very important mystical conjunction that Pentecost this year fell on the day of the Crescent Moon, and we were most anxious that you should restate your Vow under the perfect ray of the Crescent Moon so that you should be more protected in the times to come. You may not see now all the implications of that protection, but be assured that it is most important. You will only realise the importance later. But in your unconscious selves great things are being achieved tonight that will be completed in your sleep. These will be my last words tonight. Your Master is here. He has an important message to deliver but first He bids me tell you that you should think of the others who are not here and include them in your attentive obedience to His words. So is the great angel present with you tonight. He who is the Lord of your destiny.

☙❀❧

August 1946
Thalia and Ninon — through Ninon

Build sanctuaries that should extend from the sands of Palestine to the shores of the Pacific in a chain of havens where the weary may rest their heads and the sinner wash his sins. It is the cosmic echo of the first chain of chapels built by My faithful as they scattered to the four winds to bring My message to those who needed to be awakened from their age-long sleep. Mind you, I say chapels not churches. Chapels are the heart and core of religion. The churches are its arms, and it is easier to tempt the arms to grab than to spoil the core. The arms are falling to pieces by the side of senseless bodies. But in the heart still lies enshrined the Star of Bethlehem. From these sparks when the time comes will spring a mighty fire that will illumine the world.

Verily I say unto you, blessed are you among women, that

because you once held the Chalice you have been called to see the spark of the Holy Spirit. This is the message that comes to you at the approach of the full moon, in the chapel of the birds, dedicated to the one who was the most loving of all men [St. Francis], who, because of that great love, has the greatest harvest of blessings to spread on this madness-driven world. Peace be unto you.

❧❖❧

October 7th, 1946
the Studio, Rake Manor, Godalming, Thalia's home
Thalia and Ninon — through Ninon

Blessings, blessings, the Lord is here, your Lord pouring his Love over your shattered bodies as great miracles are due to happen soon. This is a holy place of retreat, and verily I say unto you, those who today have no place of retreat are greatly to be pitied. The world has become such a place of walking evil that souls shake and shiver in its midst. All those called upon to survive, as they have been awakened to the higher life, must have places of retreat, where they can find peace and see clearly.

Unto the sands of the desert are gathering clouds of sorrow. From there the fire will strike as lightning and the sparks will spread over the earth for the final battle. Gather, O soldiers of peace for the greatest battle ever fought by mankind.

All My saints and My disciples have been reawakened for the immense struggle. That is why the old signs have to come to life again and the Grail and the stone have to be found and seen. Nothing can tear away the Light in My children's eyes, once they have seen the Cup of Peace and Love which blossomed from My sorrow and sacrifice. Unto you both I give the power to see. I bless you and gather you to My mantle of love as in the days gone by which have started anew. Peace and Love

❧❖❧

October 9th 1946
the Studio, Rake Manor, Thalia and Ninon

Those who are born to sing must sing, otherwise they will never know happiness, but their songs, if they have seen the beauties hidden beyond the world, must be in praise of the Unique One, the Lord of our Love and our happiness, the Saviour of our souls and the Healer of our minds.

You must try to imagine as you go to sleep, that you slumber on a cloud of roses whose perfume will linger long after the memory of your senses fades. This is an excellent purification and a way to ensure restful sleep. All the disharmony of the world must be laid to rest before the elect can rest themselves without being overladen with the cares of the astral realm.

The discipline of creation with all its pain is a discipline we must learn. The eternal quest must come to its goal. The time has come when the truth must be brought to bear, not only on the minds of the elect, but also impress with its blessings, those who are on the right track. The Lord, our Lord, is coming closer to the earth in order to re-establish order in his lost bewildered church. What lies buried in the bowels of the earth or enshrined in Heaven must be seen again by those who are awakened to the eternal realities of life. Asraf

❧❀❧

October 9th, 1946
The Studio, Rake Manor,
Thalia and Ninon — through Ninon

Blessings, blessings, blessings, My dearest beloved daughters, at last on the long Way of Love have you come to My embrace again in the burning revelation of My hidden trust. This is a church and an altar. Here you must pray for My eternal service. Verily I say unto you, upon the sands of Jerusalem lies the cloud of woe. The betrayer has again achieved his end, but for My true followers the Light of the Cup that has arisen is a flaming power. Press it to your heart that it will ever more burn there, as a jewel of love and heavenly joy. This is a mystical marriage. You should be immersed in joy. I have come to you that you may kneel and pray as those who have faithfully accomplished their pilgrimage and have found Me waiting for them at the end. Bare your heart, give it to Me and I will bring it in safe custody to its heavenly shrine. Love, Love, Love to you, faithful retrieved daughters of My Living Word.

ৡৄ❀ৡৄ

October 10th, 1946 — Full moon
Thalia and Ninon, through Ninon

It is very important to know the difference between the Law of Nature and the law of the world. The great mistake of the Church was to try and suppress the Law of Nature. Our nature — as long as it respects Nature — is right and true. We have to live in Nature. It reflects the Law of Heaven. Hidden behind the first Church there was to have been an image of heaven, symbolised by the dome of the Church. Christ usually preached in Nature. It must start that way again. **Every act of a human being must be judged according to these rules: does it offend Nature? Does it offend God? Does it injure Life?**

Each man or woman has to build again his or her own sanctuary. One of the dangers on the path is that as each group to which the truth has been given passes on, dogmatism can take over. We must consciously choose to do God's Will on earth. Nature does this unconsciously. What is difficult is not to live according to the Will of God when one knows the Will of God. The easiest thing to do is to live by it.

To live the Will of God is the secret of happiness as there is no possibility of disharmony. The temptation lies not in fact but in illusion. The senses are the servants of illusion, as long as they are not made the channels of the Will of God. This is the secret of artistic creation, and the stone which was a rose and the essence of My Blood.

Transfiguration is the greatest mystery on earth. Those who understand it are struck by the grace of God whose deepest meaning lies in the miracle of the Transfiguration. Raise what we think we see to the level where it reflects the image of what we are meant to see under the law of God.

Meditate on this, My daughters, and you will come nearer to the truth of heaven than you have ever been before in this life, where you had to be born with many lost memories. To regain them was to show the way to those who had never seen them, even in past lives. Remember that My Way is the way of Life even if it passes through the forests of death, because the Will of God is happiness even if we discover it through suffering. The image beyond the Earth is the star that should guide our acts and give them the deepest meanings. Verily, verily, I say unto you, those who believe in the laws of the world will die even if they live and those who believe in the laws of God and follow My way will live even if they die.

❧✿☙

Pentecost 1947
Thalia and Ninon — through Ninon

Peace be unto you. Gather in the remembrance of the upper room where I spoke the words of the Last Supper. Make your minds clear and your hearts pure of any evil thoughts. Verily, verily, I say unto you, the time has come when the power of thought is to be recognised and the evil thoughts of man will come crashing back on him like a burning torch. The time has come when not only by actions but by the thoughts that determine them will man be judged and placed in his rightful place in the scale of evolution.

The former Pentecost was a feast of action. The Pentecost of the New Age will be one of thought. Because thought is action, and action without thought is bread without leaven. Too long has man tried to hide his actions behind thoughtlessness, yet when he saw the havoc his actions caused, he cried out helplessly "O Lord, I did not mean to do any of this" but verily I say unto you tonight and this must be repeated, the time has come when the Lord will say "Man, you are responsible being, did I give you thought for you to act like a small child or an animal in dismay?" No. You must know that before man can be redeemed in his evolution, he has first to clear his thoughts and live as if they were an open mirror in which everyone could read and decipher. The spiritual dawn that is nearing will make this evident to each one of the chosen who will live to see it grow today. Each must have his conscience clear on the day of reckoning or he will not be able to survive.

When I say conscience, do not misunderstand me. I mean that no one should cheat himself and live according to two laws — the law of his thought and the law of his action. Both must be subservient to an inner harmony which can only be gathered from the cosmos or from an inner understanding of the superior law of God. It will be the foundation of the Church of the New Age, the one that is to be built on the invisible stone that I have already talked to you about.

At Pentecost the gift of understanding was given to My disciples and also the knowledge and the science that they did not have to learn in order to know, because science and learning were important at that moment. Yet such purity of heart was necessary to the spreading of My faith that I could not stop and choose My disciples among the learned of the day. I had to give them learning through the intuition that is divine and the spark of the Holy Ghost.

Today at Pentecost knowledge has to be raised to a superior level of thought where it will again join the divine intuition, but this time intuition will not descend. It is knowledge which through the power of thought will have to be raised to the level of intuition. This may seem a little hard for you to understand today but later the realisation of this deep truth will come to you easily. This is the message of Pentecost which I had in store for you. About the secret of the stone which is at the same time a flower [a rose] and the essence of My blood I will speak to you later, when you are in southern France. There will be a great deal for you to understand there, a great deal of experience for you to go through which will enable you to start your mission well-prepared. Peace be on you, My daughters. I have spoken.

ஐ❋ஐ

September 29th, 1947
[time of The Partition of India]
Thalia and Ninon

Under the sign of the full moon, we greet you, children of the living word. Do not despair if some of our words escape your understanding. You can meditate on what you do not know. You can grasp the essence even if it is above the level of your logical minds. There are many doors opening, secret doors of heaven; and faithful concentration is one of the ways. You must realise that souls can be blinded by the uncovering of the perfect light before they have attained perfect maturity, just as the human eye can be blinded by light that is too strong for its limited capacity. Yet the light exists and is not less strong because it is shrouded.

Into Michael's hands has been delivered the task of saving what is to be saved of this planet. You are now commanded to work under Michael's orders as you have become his soldiers, soldiers of peace: peace within the mind, peace beneath the heart; peace within and without because without peace there can be no further life. The call is urgent, as now on our plane, the work has been done and the orders given. It is the same with us as with those living on earth: there are mistakes and failures. Now that through Michael, order has been restored on our side, we can now come through and give our orders.

In the near future, there will be no immediate war, but crisis after crisis that will completely upset the human mind and cause it to shatter the frame of organised civilisation. You can see the signs of these coming disturbances in what is happening in

India and in Palestine. For no logical reason blood is being shed and more will follow, if those whose minds are still sound do not react and react openly. Very soon must those who work in secret come out into the open and tell what they know. It is our wish and we will make it known. In the meantime, we bid you welcome in the band of the appointed fighters for the truth and peace. This is the new crusade. God and Christ are with us. Asraf

September 29th, 1947 continued...

Peace be with you; Peace to the East, the West, the South and the North. As the Prince of Peace, I speak with you and I say, verily, verily, there is to be no peace as the germs of truth have again been shut away in the bowels of the earth. Yet everywhere My faithful are gathered, awaiting My orders. To them I say be ready, for the new struggle has begun. More devastating weapons than the splitting elements are being worked upon in secret; forces powerful enough to reverse the laws of Nature. The danger lies in the East and in the West.

Under the Archangels, legions of the heavenly host are being trained to serve humanity. The core of the evil lies in the East, near the sands of Palestine. The wanton thirst to kill will be aroused more and more, so pray that your mind be lifted above the vibration of the suffering Earth. For only those who have that ability will be able to resist the madness that will be the fourth horseman of this time.

Be on the lookout for the invisible church and prepare maps of all the holy places you have found and try to link them in thought. It is when the visible church will have crashed down under the assaults of its own sons that the invisible church must be ready to appear before despairing humanity as the star of hope. Verily, verily, I say unto you, you will see this day, so be grateful and remember that faith is to the soul what the health of the bones is to the body. Peace, Peace, Peace.

❧❀☙

September 30, 1947
Thalia and Ninon — through Ninon

There are periods which seem to be lasting forever. They are periods of incubation. Everything today is in a state of waiting. The dice are thrown but the pieces have not yet been moved. The two great forces of Light and of Darkness are being gathered. Everywhere on this planet the call for action has gone forth. Greater and more terrible discoveries than the splitting of the atom are being hatched in secret. All those who were disciples of our Lord in the past have been tested to see in what capacity they can best serve the Lord of Liberation who will ensure the New Age.

The breaking up of the established churches is but a question of time. It will be partly accomplished their own inability to satisfy the spiritual needs of man, and partly by the action of the atheists [communists and materialists] who will play a greater and greater part in world events. Everywhere centres are being built on former holy ground, so that even if communications should be disrupted due to prevailing world conditions, enough links will have already been established so that the future initiates can communicate with other initiates by the power of thought and of prayer. It is a task of My master to awaken those centres and to bring back those signs, whose meaning has been forgotten, and which lie as if enshrined in their own graves, and restore them to life again. That is why He is trying so hard to awaken memories of past revelations in the minds of those disciples who can hearken to His words today.

Beware of the sands of Palestine. That is where the biggest trouble in the world lies today, and there is the centre of the Anti-Christ. All those who will be involved with the work of this enemy of man will run a terrible danger. He will only be conquered by the fire of the Grail but before undertaking this new crusade, people will have to go through the experience of the new Pentecost as it was described to you, and that of the Siege Perilous. Read what is said in the Arthurian legend about the eve of Pentecost, and the meaning it had for those of King Arthur's Court. A miracle always happened at Pentecost and it is the unexpected which becomes the law on the higher plane.

It is the intention of our Lord that you should try to unify knowledge and intuition. You are on the intuitive side of humanity. Seek those who have practical knowledge, and try to make them understand that they need to work with those who have intuition. No longer can humanity bear to be split by the prevailing conflict. Harmony has to be found again so that man can be saved from his own destructive civilisation. The next victim on the scroll of the Anti-Christ is not the body of man, as everything has been prepared for its destruction, but the mind of man. There is the danger of collective insanity.

From the seventeenth century, man's mastery of Nature became more and more developed and the idea of power gradually became identified with the idea of man's power over matter and Nature, which led eventually to the splitting of the atom and the splitting of the human psyche. Before we leave a technical age where power has been limited to power over matter, to be ushered into a New Age where intuition and mystical power will have to be developed again, it is essential that man should learn to discipline his thoughts as he now does his body through sport. Or what we face is the material destruction of the earth.

Only those who have reached an inner harmony between their feeling and their faith, their knowledge and their intuition; their thoughts and their actions; those who live according to the Law of Nature and the Law of God, as already explained, can hope to save their fellow men and be able to say the right word at the right moment. Do not be of little faith because, if you are willing and obedient, the strength will be given to you when you need strength. What is important is the willingness to listen to the voice of the guidance within your heart which tells you which way to go and what to say. Those who are able to listen and accept the guidance of their heart will be given the strength to help their fellow men. Is not Pentecost a miracle? As the gift of language was given to those who had to speak to spread the Faith, so will come the strength that is lacking now, when the moment arrives. The blessing of the Lord.

June 4th, 1948
The Studio, Rake Manor,
Thalia and Ninon — through Ninon

Peace be unto you. Peace, daughters of the Living Word. What I taught you in the past must now be assimilated by you and come out as statements, symbols and facts. For, as the good seed planted in the heart must blossom at harvest time, so must My Word planted in you, grow, blossom, and bear fruit. You have been given more to learn than most mortals in their time of earthly exile. This is not due to your present merit, for you were born feeble and erroneous in many ways, but due to your past experience with Me as My servants. Sometimes the strongest egos have to take the weakest personalities so as to show the world of their time the way to redemption through their example. For there are as many ways to spiritual achievements as there are doors to the city of God. The way of learning is one of them. The way of redemption is another.

With the breaking down of most of the established faiths, and particularly of the one I opened the way to, the human soul, having lost its shield, stands weak and shuddering at the threshold of truth.

Many a wise man or woman has tried to open the closed gate, but verily, verily, I say unto you today, it is through the intuition of the weak that the light will be found again, not through the will of the strong. So do not despair if you still feel the weakness of your human self. It is all to the good, for by such will the way be shown, and it is My wish that you should work now with those many who have been deceived by the Church and who are now like boats riding the seas without proper sails. Unto your hands and the hands of My other faithful, I have delivered the sails which come from the wings of My angels that have time after time led the chosen to the harbour of peace.

Build around you a wall of light so that you stay protected from the foul emanations of this earth. See it spread around you as a blazing shield when you speak, paint, or write.

For verily I say unto you that only those who are as protected as were the knights on the quest of the Grail can rediscover among the perils and temptations of the world, the Cup of Harmony and the Crown of My Blessing. I extend My hands in blessing over your heads, that My Peace may descend on your brow, your throat, and your heart. Peace, Peace, Peace.

❧❀❧

May 1st, 1949
Rake Manor, Godalming, Surrey — Thalia and Ninon

If you re-read the teachings of the past years, you will acquire a new understanding of your messages. We had to surprise you with them at the time, so as to give the stream of your consciousness the shock that was necessary to set it flowing in the right direction. Now we ask you to understand them and to put them into action. As I told you, your way lies with the world, and you will have to tackle its problems and dive your hands into its sufferings. You are not meant now to follow the way of meditation and solitary soliloquy with the spiritual realm.

I must tell you that those who are dedicated to the incarnation of heavenly things in time and space must give great care to the body when their soul is doing this kind of work. Perfect physical condition is necessary to the accomplishment of work like yours. Only after this period of looking after your body will you be free to go on with your work. We are well pleased with you, but you must still acquire more mental poise. You must not let people swirl you around as the wind does the flowers and the trees. You are required only to obey the heavenly wind of spiritual vision. Show a smiling face to the world. Your smile is your strength. Go your way with your hand outstretched to receive our help. You need independence. If you set your mind to this aim, your life from now on can be made much smoother. It is in you to obtain this peace. What we want from you is the expression in your time and space of what is eternal, indivisible and holy.

Your Friend between the two worlds, Asraf.

May 11th, 1953
Pentecost, Thalia and Ninon — through Ninon

Peace be unto you, My daughters; Peace be unto you. That which often seems to be contradictory is only due to the limitation of your understanding. Mental intelligence is of use to help you to manage the details of your practical lives as human beings. It is not the same kind of intelligence as that which is needed to contemplate the Essence of Divine Nature. The more you progress, the more you should shed the limitations of division and separation and open yourselves to the Oneness of God.

The mystery of the Trinity was one of the symbols used by the Father, by Me and by the Holy Spirit, to express the understanding that man, who in his essence is God, is never alone in the contemplation of Divinity — Divinity which is also himself, the Eternal. He needs to understand that the other is also himself, in the everlasting understanding of things. The emphasis put on the Son as the Redeemer was one of the mistakes made by My Church in the narrowing into dogma, of the truth that I tried to give as inspiration, and not as admonition.

We are coming to the age where the Holy Spirit is the incarnation of God. We should particularly dedicate ourselves to it as it is the most impersonal.

> The first Age is that of the Father.
> The second Age is that of the Son.
> The third Age is that of the Holy Spirit.

It is only through humanity that man can solve the problem of his inhumanity. Like children, men tamper with the laws of Nature, trying to bend them to their presumptuous purposes. He who uses the sword in spite of the Law of God, will perish by the sword. He who uses the fire of God in spite of the Law of God, will perish by the fire of God. Already we see the results around us of man's presumptuous endeavour to use the elements of matter, not for beneficial purposes, but for destruction. [nuclear weapons]

It is the karmic responsibility of America to have in its

power mighty knowledge to which the necessary wisdom has not yet been added. That is why so much of the dark forces are at work there at the moment. The next battle will be on the inner plane. The danger is not immediate in the material world but it is looming closer spiritually.

Insinuating rays are spreading from the places where scientists are doing experiments, which affect human bodies and human minds, creating a state of splitting psyches, which on the human plane is what the splitting of energy is on the cosmic plane. Only by lifting his consciousness to a higher level of unity and awareness of Oneness can man escape his doom and acquire the wisdom rightly to use the power over Nature that his intelligence has given him. This power is only beneficial through the application of wisdom, otherwise it risks becoming all-destroying.

Verily, verily, I say unto you, My daughters, we are treading on more dangerous ground than that which led to the Cross where you saw Me, because all that I had to accomplish in My First Coming was the symbolism through death and resurrection of the lasting power of man to survive physical death and to achieve his salvation through brotherhood with his fellow man. The followers of My cause had to fear the destruction of their bodies but they had in their souls the vision of My resurrection. Many of them passed directly into the Glory of God without having to undergo the pain of any change of state.

But, now, My daughters, no single person can show the way. It is through the collective work of many that the way can be found. We have to move from personal salvation to cosmic salvation. Each must work for himself but at the same time work for the others so that each centre becomes one of a group of effective sources of goodness and vision that work on the general principle of an electric dynamo. When the dynamo works, all the centres are lit up, and the Light is One and Universal, be it here, or in France or Russia. But sometimes, because the darkness is greater, or the need to see the Wisdom of God is greater, one of the centres may receive more light than another.

Gather people where you are, write many letters and pray to the Holy Spirit.

Blessed are those who see behind and beyond the veils of separateness into the realms of Divine Unity. Blessed are the souls, the minds and the spirits of those who seek the Light of Oneness in the contemplation of the Divine Ground beyond the shadows of space and time.

❧ ✿ ☙

Pentecost 1953
Thalia and Ninon — through Ninon

I am the Light and the Wine and the Bread!

Behold and Hark!

I am treading among the heavenly fields, but out of my heart's overflowing love to you My brethren, and My flock, I extend My hands in blessings and say,

Come to me —
The time has come
Come to me —
The time is near
So that My Second Coming may come to pass.
Only through awareness and longing from you to Me can I bring you, My Brethren and My flock, the blessing of the millennium.

In the name of the Christ
of the Son
and the Holy Spirit

I welcome you on the threshold of the New Church, the Church of Light whose doors are transparent stone. Its pillars extend upwards like lilies, raising their petals to the kiss of Divine Compassion. Its altar is the stone which received My Blood and made it into a flower whose perfume, like incense, filled the nostrils of those who age after age made their life the Quest of the Absolute.

Behold My Church and be welcomed into it! You will see there My disciples and My Saints, not in portraits or as statues but smiling at you in the clothing of their heavenly bodies. Among them smile the patron of regenerated Nature, your loving Francis, and St. George and the glorious Michael.

My Church rises like a ladder to the Heavenly Glories of the Father, whose wisdom made this world through the Word and the Law. Visit this Church in the silence so that the memory may always be with you and so this vision may stay in your hearts to give it strength and happiness. Keep the strength within you and proclaim the happiness, and may your hands, your lips, and your words be blessed with the power to proclaim the TRUTH that I have by this vision unfolded before your eyes. Go, PRAISE GOD and say with all your heart and soul ALLELUIA, ALLELUIA. THE LORD IS WITH US.

Nothing is ours that is not first of God. It is to be blessed with the understanding and contemplation of Essences that I have called you together tonight.

This is the gift of Pentecost and this is the gift that I give to you tonight.

On the cross I gave up three things to the cause of humanity.

My sweat
My blood
and My Spirit

I gave them up humanly so that by following My lead man in his progress towards God, could discover the mysteries of these three ways to eternal resurrection.

The sweat is the sacrifice of the body to the Cause of Nature. By sweat does man unite with the miracle of Nature and penetrates to the essence of the mineral and vegetable worlds.

By My blood which blossomed in the Grail which is both flower and stone, the animal world became transmuted into the Divine World of which the Spirit is the key.

The Spirit comes third and last of the Trinity. It is the Ancient

Logos. It is expressed in the Word of Power. Those who follow the Holy Spirit see God and speak with the Eternal Spirit. The personality is then raised into the unity of the Divine Monad, and the mind of each and every one is able to see things beyond time and space.

❧ ✿ ☙

October 4th, 1953
Thalia and Ninon — through Ninon

Blessings on you, children of My Living Word — for in the true understanding of My Word is everlasting life and the key to My Kingdom. I have come to show the Way, which is One, although it can be reached by many different paths.

Today I want to teach you the meaning of Blessings, and give you the power to learn their ritual use. Blessing provokes and achieves the state of bliss which is harmony. Without harmony there is no bliss. The gesture of blessing is the ritual of harmony.

There is the power to bless where there is the ability to live selflessly, that is, without the desire to possess and acquire, which always means destruction by absorption of the object of love.

Love that blesses gives. Bliss is the love that expands; it is not the love the demands.

Look at Nature and you will find two forces at work: the force of love that blesses and gives, where the flower gives its beauty and the tree its strength. And there is the force that takes away and destroys. This is the great test of our time, where control over Nature has almost been reached by man through his mastery of technology.

If this is used for love and for blessing it will make the Aquarian Age the Age of the fulfilment of My Coming, and verily the true millennium. But if it is used for malediction and for hate, then the catastrophe will be upon us and this will be the equivalent of cosmic suicide. If you mix the waters of knowledge with the thought of destruction, then destruction will come. The Water-bearer who showed the way to the house where I took leave of My disciples in My then body, is showing the way again.

Use blessings for the blessed ritual of love, then will their soft waves bring beauty and harmony to the planet which, with the infinite possibilities of this Age, will transform it into a new heaven on earth, as it was in the time when it was called the earthly Paradise. For the time of fulfilment has come. Even those who deny Me, know that if the Earth does not become like a Paradise, it will become one of those wrecked planets that wander as ruins in the darkened cosmos.

To you and those like you, I want to give the teaching and the knowledge of the things to come so that you may build My armies of love, whose centres and groups become like a precious fortress which guards My Kingdom. You can, by concentration, meditation, and the humility of prayer, learn to use the force of blessing in your word, your gesture, your drawings, your writings, your approach to other human beings. It will come to you gradually.

It is a great strength.

It can perform miracles when developed wisely, so never abuse it, or will turn against you. I will show you gradually the use of it and, in your turn, you will teach it to others.

Verily, verily, I say unto you, this is a precious holy gift, that I will put into your hands in time. Receive it with faith and humility, after dedicating yourselves to its use.

And now I will leave you. My blessing unto you, and to those who are with you in thought, who labour under My banner for the establishment of My Kingdom.

***

February 25th, 1954
New York — Thalia, Ninon and Lilla — through Lilla

Everywhere on this planet the call has gone out. From far distant realms in the Universe come Great Beings to your poor benighted planet, to stand with the children of the Light in the effort to overthrow the tyranny of evil once and for all, and to triumph over it so that never again shall it overpower the world. If enough people fearlessly stand in the Light and keep it bright when the darkness would engulf it, then with this help from outer space, you shall succeed and triumph. But there is a danger that too many will be intimidated into weak compromise or indifference. See that this is not said of you. You need to become as wise as serpents and as gentle as doves.

Wake up, man. Wake up to your immortal soul or it will be taken away from you. For you must know that souls can be taken away from unworthy carriers.

❧✿☙

February 1954
New York — Thalia and Ninon — through Ninon

PEACE BE WITH US, WITHIN US AND ON THE WORLD. PEACE WITHIN AND WITHOUT SO THAT THE LIGHT OF CHRIST CAN SHINE AGAIN AND ANNOUNCE THE BEGINNING OF THE MILLENNIUM AND THE FULFILMENT OF THE SECOND COMING, FOR THE TEMPLE IS READY TO CRUMBLE, THE VEIL TO BE TORN, AND THE EARTH TO OPEN.

Sorrow upon those who see Me yet deny Me; who could touch Me, yet turn away from Me. To you, My daughters, who trod with me at the beginning of this era, I tell you that you are entering a new stage of evolution — the stage of conscious realisation of the purpose of your spiritual ascension.

You are now at the first stage of the way to the Holy Mountain. New centres are going to awaken in you. New powers will be added to the limitations of your strength because we wish to call upon you to be among the inner leaders of our armies of salvation.

Yes, before you part, the Light is going to descend and glide over your higher centres, so that you will understand things which have been obscured until now. Your eyes will open to new sights and you will be able to be fully equipped to fight against those who would prevent the fulfilment of what I prophesied when I spoke last on earth. Rest now and pray and the Blessing of the Word will touch you with its fiery touch of Light, Life and Illumination.

ᘛ❀ᘚ

February 25th, 1954
New York — Thalia and Ninon — through Ninon

Greetings, dear daughters. You are thinking along the right lines and we are rejoicing over your clairvoyance. You are now able to listen to us without having to write but your main task lies not in remembering the past but in building the future. The ability to remember is an exercise and often a test of your progress in your present incarnation but it is not a task.

Your duty towards your eternal ego is to accomplish what you have been sent to earth to accomplish in your present life. You have been given the ability to create, and create you must. You have in your keeping a spark of the Light that has to be added to the glow of the Holy Chapel I told you about in my last message to you. Many lives you two have been together and you are more closely linked than sisters or brothers because you have often been the expression of the same entity. You must try and get rid as quickly as possible all lower vibrations which hamper you still, so you can go in spirit to the Chapel and rejoice in its beauty, before bringing back to others the message of this eternal dwelling, which is, to our Age, what the church was in times past.

Never forget that evolution goes forward. You should look forward. There is much need for help as so-called progress is taking man into realms that he is not equipped to grasp spiritually. Remember what you were told about the coming catastrophe? We can reveal to you now, and for that reason you were drawn earlier this evening into a discussion about Ahriman and Lucifer. We can tell you now that we are at the top of the spiral which started with the throwing out of heaven of the presumptuous spirit. This spirit has been working from the earth outwards and has inspired all the scientific discoveries which threaten to destroy the earth. Michael is trying to help the development of the spiritual qualities which will avert this catastrophe by helping man to re-establish the balance between his free will and God by the contemplation of eternal laws. But the danger is great.

The holy Chapel is the meeting place of all the souls who work towards the salvation of this planet and the realisation of God's plan as revealed to you by Master Jesus, the Christ and the Saviour, guided by the Holy Spirit. Be on your way to the Chapel dearest daughters. We watch over you. I have spoken. Your friend between heaven and earth, Asraf.

❧❀☙

June 6th, 1954 — Pentecost

Dearest ones, Blessings on you. It is I, Asraf, your friend between heaven and earth, bringing you the flowers of Pentecost, the flowers of fire which blossom in the cup and the jewel of eternal divine love. Let your hearts expand to join with all the hearts which today revel in the great feast of understanding, which is the feast of Pentecost.

This day like every year before and every year to come, we rejoice in the understanding of the heart, uniting the third eye in us with the fire of the revelation that everything is One in the spheres beyond us, and that reunion follows separation, and incarnation in the spirit follows incarnation in the flesh.

At Pentecost a miracle always happens, as this is the higher ceremony of baptism in the opening of the understanding of the heart. Every soul is reborn at Pentecost a step further in the progress of its evolution towards its counterpart in heaven.

Let then your hearts and souls rejoice in this knowledge. Many today will be touched with this truth. It will be breathed on those chosen ones who want to go the way of the Higher Brothers who work as disciples in the spheres where I dwell.

Go and rejoice, my dearest ones, the message of Pentecost is with you. This summer many things are due to happen as this is the end of a smaller cycle within the larger cycle of the age. Meet with your sisters. The Master will speak to you of His will and make you partake of His love for you and for this suffering planet.

The blessing of the Persian angel will pour on your foreheads to open the eternal centre of your understanding of things both divine and human. You should praise joy and beauty and the lightness of heart of the soul that has shaken off its fetters. This is the great freedom that liberates the soul from the laws of gravity.

๕๕๏ฃ๑

December 1954
New York — Thalia and Ninon — through Ninon

Greetings and love, children of my heart. Your friend Asraf is with you, hovering over the higher centres of your being.

Do not waste too much energy on your daily tasks. Remember that energy is the vital principle of your body and that you are responsible for it to your higher guidance. For you, who have been chosen to carry the flame, it is indispensable for you to concentrate on those tasks that have been assigned to you in the path of your evolution. Your daily chores have to be organised, planned, and then carried out lightly, and without effort. They are to be attended to, but not given over-emphasis.

Painting is the way for Thalia to channel her energy in the higher direction. You must learn more and more to be active, yet completely detached, as without realising it, you are already in a higher cycle — the third of the levels you can consciously reach. You must dedicate your thoughts to the mental journey to the pure Chapel of the Holy Grail, the Chapel of Light where lies enthroned the Holy Grail. This is the message I wanted to give you as this is the next step you have to take on your path of progression. It seems easy, but it is not, and in the Chapel, you will find a happiness that you have not yet experienced. There you will meet old friends, pilgrims of wisdom already arrived at their goal. Rejoice, for this is a joyous experience.

You must meditate on the problem of Judas. Remember you were warned about his roving spirit. The spirit of Judas sells the birth-right of man — to reach his higher self — for purely temporal or material things, so that he forgets his true task and destiny and becomes immersed in what is not essential.

Open your palms to receive the down-pouring of my strength and on your heads, receive my blessing. Asraf

❧❦❀❦☙

Sunday after Pentecost, 1955
Thalia and Ninon — through Ninon

Blessings upon you, daughters of My Living Word, blessings to you and to the world, blessings from the Father, the Son, and the Holy Spirit.

WE SPEAK TO YOU TODAY IN THE NAME OF THE LIVING SPIRIT WHICH LIVES AND ANIMATES ALL THE PLANETARY WORLDS OF THE HIERARCHY, WITHIN AND WITHOUT.

We want to animate all your active and passive centres with the blessing of the Spirit so that you will feel awakened to all that lies within, as well as beyond, your grasp. For verily, verily, those who still sleep today will never awaken again, for this is the time of trial. You must understand that we do not want to pass judgement although this is judgement day, but simply to state that we are just within the reach of the kingdom of God.

This is the time of My Second Coming, which will not be of the flesh, but of the Spirit. I have tried to show the Way, as the light seen in the storm shows the way to the haven of peace and security, because even those who are divine, and belong to the heavenly flame, can only show man the Way. They cannot tread the Path for him. We give through symbols the Way to follow, to acquire immortality. Immortality is not a right we receive from our birth, but a privilege given by the Father to His beloved and most obedient children. Those who have heard the call of the trumpet of judgement, will forever have gained victory over that which carries the seed of destruction, which is death.

Man has made great advances in the knowledge of the universe but he has used it for his own ends and has not discovered its Eternal Divine Laws. Through the knowledge of these Laws, he would have been obliged to recognise that which is of the Father, belongs to the Father, and that which is of the Son, belongs to the Son, with the blessing of the Holy Spirit. Man needs to recognise that knowledge is sterile, and even dangerous if it is not raised beyond knowledge to the level of the wisdom of the Spirit.

What we want you to do, My daughters, who were with Me time after time, is to concentrate on the study of the Universe and the Harmony of the Cosmos within and without. For all that is true of the world and the heavens above is also true for man incarnate. You must meditate on this truth and express it to yourselves and then to others in terms which are appropriate to this age and its problems.[8]

8. The fact that each one of us is a hologram of the entire cosmos is becoming clear through quantum physics.

I sent out My disciples at Pentecost to preach the Law after I had endowed them with the intuitive knowledge of the Spirit, but what is to be preached now is so much more important and the times are so much more urgent that I have to rely, not on a small group of faithful, but on all those who have been prepared for the task, age after age, until finally they have reached this testing one.

Did it not strike you today that the Age of Aquarius is the age of Hydrogen, and the age when scientific advance has come to the point where Hydrogen may mean the destruction of this planet or its transformation into the true Elysium, or heaven on earth. Verily, verily, I say unto you, it would be better for those of this generation never to have been born, and having been born, not to become fully awakened to the moral responsibility of this dangerous yet promise-fulfilling Age which is the one of My Second Coming.

So I say to you, daughters dear to My heart, to truly meditate. Meditate on the knowledge which is coming your way every day with clearer insight, for it will be your task to make it understandable to more and more of your brethren in need of help. I will give you soon the symbols of the New Age. From now on there can be no more accidents, but only clairvoyant understanding of the planetary fate, which will consist of all the individual fates of those who have chosen to show the way from the splitting elements and their destructive power to the new Hierarchy of the Universe.

My blessing upon you now and forever, and through all Eternity, your Master.

❧❀☙

August 15th, 1956
Sherding, Austria — Thalia and Ninon — through Ninon

Greetings my daughters. I am glad to see you together, willing to work for the Plan. The need is great. We had to send a call again to all our pupils scattered over this planet, as the time has come when, more than ever, the children of Light have to assemble to create the great invisible church which will be built on the many planes of life, and will be the only protection against the destructive powers which are starting to gnaw again at the roots of this unhappy planet.

If you could only see from our side what is on the way to happening again, you would be appalled and horrified. That is why you are not allowed to see it as you are not ready yet. We want you to pray and to meditate, to try and raise your vibrations throughout this day so that we can start teaching you tonight, leading you to a higher plane of consciousness which you must have for the great revelation which is in store for you.

Remember that contacts are not to be sought from personal

motives, but people who work honestly and earnestly to raise the veil in order to help humanity and to obey the call of their guardians in the process of doing their work. These are given the privilege of meeting their loved ones and are able to find again that community of thought and action which had given them happiness in previous lives. But only through selflessness and humility can these higher contacts be achieved, and be helpful to those who are striving to come together on the borders between the visible and the invisible worlds. If you push the veil aside through your personal wishes, it will soon fall again, thicker than ever.

But if you throw it aside through earnest work and striving, it will stay forever open for you, and while still in your denser body, you can enjoy the use of the higher centres, which generally are not open to those still in their fleshly garments.

Our Blessing and our Love. Asraf

August 20th, 1956
Richesberg, Austria — Thalia and Ninon — through Ninon

The Divine Mother is the Holy Spirit who presides over the New Age. Only water and its healing strength can extinguish the over-riding fires of Mars. Inspired by her, women, through their love and understanding, have been given the task of awakening in men the compassion and brotherly love taught by Me at the beginning of the Piscean Age. Man, through woman, will realize in himself the sense of his mission on earth and see clearly as in a mirror, the law of the universe. When that time comes, the secrets of Nature will be understood.

The Divine Mother has been prepared for ages for the time when, according to the stars, she will be the Mother of all those who would willingly drink of the Cup of Sorrow, to be carried into heaven on the wings of the eternal principle of Love and Compassion.

This is the great privilege that was given to the Western world with My coming, to be able to have always near them and above them, the Divine Mother. It is the initiation through the heart centre which combined with the initiation of the higher centre of the brain, will bring the evolved ones of this planet to the complete realisation of God's plan within them and within the Universe. The Holy Mother will be the Redeemer of the New Age because she will take everything upon herself and, like the alchemist of the Middle Ages, will transform and fuse the harder elements in the surging waters of compassionate Love. Only she can re-establish the great Equilibrium between the destructive forces and the ever-building principle of Life and Love.

❧❀☙

August 23rd, 1956 — Neuberg, Austria

They [Thalia and Ninon] had been told to go to the Grotto to awaken their centres. It had been raining all day. On the way there they saw a marvellous black and gold lizard and a slug, and on the way back a toad. Later they were told that this lizard was not a lizard but a royal salamander, which was a very rare animal of alchemical significance. It was large, black, with wonderful bright orange patches on it. They went to the grotto and sat on the bench and got the following message:

The Virgin Mary, the Holy Maid of Nazareth, lent her body willingly to the Holy Mother to be overshadowed by her as Master Jesus was overshadowed by the Christ, as the Buddha's mother was overshadowed also. This is the greatest sacrifice of the self — to become the instrument of another Being of the heavenly spheres. All those who have performed this miracle within themselves are forever liberated, and are from then on, the great transmitters of the Ray of Compassion, as they come down willingly for the sake of others and, by their sacrifice, feed that great Ray.

They were told to go and stand near the fountain and each

one of them was to baptise the other in the name of the Holy Mother and her Divine Son. "Pray and meditate and you will get your message." They stood there, not seeing any fountain. Suddenly there was a terrific noise and beneath them a torrent of water gushed forth. They rushed down to where it was, and baptised each other as ordered. Then they walked back after lighting the candle in front of the grotto where the statue of the Virgin was. They knelt and prayed to the Holy Mother. They returned, feeling lighter than angels. Suddenly they heard two birds speaking to them like the bird in the opera Siegfried, one emitting a little call, the other answering with a soft whistle. Everything seemed more beautiful. The red carpet under the pines, and the pink begonias were the most beautiful flowers they had ever seen. And then they had a message:

Do not feel disturbed, dearest daughters. This great beauty that you are seeing everywhere is only a faint reflection of the beauties of Heaven. It is now your privilege to see it everywhere, and you may sing of it, speak of it and paint it, because you will be dazzled by it yourselves. You are servants of the Lord and it is the Lord who is working through your trembling hands, and many things which have been kept from you will now become clear and evident, as it was for the great saint of Assisi who was one of the great initiates allowed to see the hidden beauties of the Universe.

You were sent three of the so-called ugly animals of creation, and yet you saw their beauty, because you saw God's patterning in this lowly form and were raised to a higher understanding of their significance. From now on you must bathe in brotherly love and heavenly beauty, and become forever members of the great White Lodge of the Lord. Miracles will become part of your daily life. Guard them preciously and give them out when you can but never forget that for those in whom the eternal eye has not yet awakened, they will still be unintelligible. You must mention these things guardedly but easily — never all at once or you could blind, drown or stifle those who are not yet ready. Remember that a tree must grow from a seed. Plant the seed in good earth and it will grow, ripen and bloom.

Blessed by the waters of the Holy Mother, entrusted with the Cup, you have become true Water Carriers. Everything you will touch with water, if you repeat the words of power, will be blessed and healed: flowers, animals, human souls. But you must use this power sparingly, knowing that wherever you are, destruction cannot come.

Now, I will give you the words of power: "Blessed are Thy Heavenly drops, O Holy Mother of Heaven. Let them carry Thy Blessings ever forth, and give Beauty, Healing and Compassion to whoever touches them in Thy Name."

Thalia realised that the Holy Mother was the Holy Spirit. She was told that a book must be written on the Queen of Heaven.

They were told about the danger to the waters of the world created by atomic explosions: The Holy Mother weeps over the profanation and pollution of Her healing waters caused by these explosions, and her tears drop as crystals on your souls, awakening them to the understanding of the great threat. Hark to Her lament and realise its meaning. Because, after the waters, will come the stars, disturbed in their rhythmic cosmic dance by the Cosmic Ray. The stars will weep with the angels, and their tears will fall as fiery sparks upon this planet. Blinded humans will say, "See the wrath of God." But from God's immanence, no wrath. It is the deformed reflection of their misdeeds that humans refuse to understand, and therefore mistakenly interpret as the wrath of God.

Hark, hark to the Song of Divine Compassion, and pray, pray with all of us, that Darkness shall not be stronger than Light, Hate stronger than Love, and that the Water-bearer shall not carry poisonous fumes in the clear pure drops of his marvellous vase.

In splitting the atom, we have become our brother's keeper. We have fragmented what was whole and are responsible for each fragment.

You must create gardens where you will protect the purity of Nature and protect the birds as well. People will come to these garden-chapels to inhale the peace.

November 13th, 1956
New York — Thalia and Ninon — through Ninon

The outpouring of Cosmic Love is overwhelming the world. The vibrations are so intense that for those who are not awake, the confusion increases. They are bombarded from all sides by an intensification of every passing thought, wish or need. The stronger cosmic rays that are pouring over this planet will affect people in two different ways. Either these rays will awaken their higher centres and enable them to develop higher gifts — clairaudience, clairvoyance — latent memories, and raise their consciousness to a higher level. Or they will affect the lower centres and create diseases like cancer — which is essentially a spiritual sickness — schizophrenia, obsession, and all the forms of insanity which are now afflicting the human race. There is no middle way at this time. Either you awake to spiritual life or you become more or less insane. To remain insulated so that these rays can only reach your higher centres is what you must try to do. You must be three times as calm, serene, healthy, as otherwise the strain might break you.

Much is happening that you cannot understand [the Hungarian Uprising] but under the confusion, the pattern and the events are unfolding as we expected them to. You who know so much, must know that no blood is ever shed in vain and that he who lays down his life for his brother is forever helped.

❧❀❧

December 8th, 1956

Greetings and blessings, daughters of the Living Word. We have brought you together to prepare you for the momentous task ahead of you. Yes, you have been chosen since the beginning of this Age and this is your most important incarnation since the one you had at the Master's feet, when you trod with Him the sands of Palestine. In the evolution of this planet, this is the most important Age since the one that started with the birth of our Lord. For centuries we have prepared souls for the miracle of this Age — His Second Coming to our earth plane to bring us with Him to the Elysian Fields of the promised Millennium.

Do not wonder, as there is still much that is beyond your grasp, but your eyes are opening and your ears becoming more and more attuned to the higher vibrations of the world beyond. There is much to tell and so little time, that we must go straight to essentials. Discard all doubt, and put your hand firmly in ours, as this is the age of miracles come to the earth and its unbelieving inhabitants. Only those who have faith can survive, that is proceed in their evolution without the setback of losing their identity.

Imagine this time as a gigantic examination set on cosmic lines with the Guardians, the Archangels, and the Elder Brethren as judges. This is not by any means the Last Judgement, but it is a Judgement Day all the same, as every soul is going to be called to testify to its progress during the last 2000 years and be called to account. Those who pass will be accepted. And those who fail will have to start all over again. The reason that you see clashes all over the world is that they always precede the Day of Judgement, the one that is about to come before our Master can gather us to his bosom and call us His children before His Father's throne. You must know that beyond all the discoveries in the realm of the atom lies the work of the Holy Spirit. It must be understood that the work must be done in His name so that the results be beneficial and not destructive and suicidal on the planetary level.

Remember all the legends about the curious, the frivolous, the un-cautious who venture unprepared beyond the veil which is called Mystery, but which is indeed a protection for those who are not yet attuned or prepared for the entrance into higher realms. They all tell of the destruction of these over-curious and unprepared careless sons of humanity. Only through the Son of Man, and under the protection of the Holy Spirit, can these realms be entered into.

The same story is repeated in our day and age and that is why we are warning all our children to be cautious in the use of their finer vehicles into which their consciousness is slowly passing, discarding the denser body of yesterday. Yes, you are a creation for the future, and that is why such high demands are made upon you. What we want from you is to meditate on these truths night and day until they become part of you. Then you will be ready for the great work ahead. Do not be frightened. We never ask the impossible and always make sure that the vehicle is prepared before we ensoul it with the Holy Spirit.

The Great Lady of Compassion [The Holy Mother] is already inspiring you, blowing into your aura the divine breath of her all-embracing love for you. You will have to lead, to inspire, to pray and to heal. Be with each other always, if not in the body, at least in the spirit. You both need the other and we can work better when you are together, but strong links forged at regular intervals can ensure the communications and keep open the channel between you, even if you are not actually in physical contact. Always imagine the channel between you with, in its midst the Cup of Light in which is mirrored the radiant light of the Son, reflecting to the Father the wonder of His creation, made through the Power of the Holy Spirit. Your friend between Heaven and Earth. Asraf

Prayer to be said every morning:

We entreat the, O Lord our Saviour,
Let thy hand rest in compassion on this shattered world.
Bend Thy radiant brow towards us, Thy children,
   still tottering in darkness.
We pray to Thee
We entreat Thee
Give us the force to resist our enemies.
Give us strength, Thy strength, that we may call Thee,
And, in Thy name, banish the evil threatening this planet.
In Thy name, and in the name of the Father,
We entreat thee,
We pray to thee, bless us, and with us all those who, in love,
   and in faith await Thy coming in the blazing LIGHT of the
   everlasting SUN. So be it.

ॐ❀ॐ

December, 1956
New York — Thalia and Ninon — through Ninon

Greetings, my daughter. It is I, Asraf. I greet you and I will stay with you for a little while. Remember to always treasure the link between you. It must be made stronger every day and especially with every night that passes. Always keep the image of the Cup of Light shining as a star between you. Always open to the outpouring love of your Master.

Your task from now on will be more and more to go into the open and contact other people. You have gathered many treasures. Now you must give them away to others. Always remember, even in the most indifferent activities of your daily life that you are the daughters of the Lord, and that you must behave as one chosen for so holy a filiation.

To learn is important but to give is still more important because we do not want you to become like the miser who accumulates his treasure in a jewelled casket and who forgets that there are others who are hungry and thirsty for even a glimpse of the treasure he has hidden.

For a long time, it was our wish that knowledge and insight should be kept in the hands of a very few on whom secrecy had been imposed. It is no more so, because, as you can see for yourselves, the way of Science and Religion have to come together if this world is to survive. That is why so many scientists are being impressed with religious thoughts and why religious people are turning to science for what was, in past ages, confined to the realm of revelation.

What was hidden at the beginning of the last Age has to come out into the open at the dawn of the New Age.

As has been taught to you by your Master, one of the first consequences of the raising of consciousness, will be a greater continuity in memory and the possibility of spanning more lives than just the present incarnation. Eventually, man will be able to live in eternity and in time simultaneously. It will be a question of accelerating or slowing down the rate of his vibrations. This may seem strange to you but stranger things have happened in the last fifty years: things which at the time you were born would have seemed impossible to the so-called intelligent people of that time.

❧❀❧

December 10th, 1956
New York — Thalia and Ninon — through Ninon

Peace be unto you. Here I am in the midst of you, extending My hands in blessing over your head, that you may see the Truth, over your throat, that you may speak the Truth, and over your heart that you may be illumined with the Love which can move mountains and overthrow the armies of the enemy of man.

Verily, verily, I say unto you, the time is near when you will see me again. Already My angels and My disciples are gathering, taking up bodies as they may need them, to do My work, on Earth. I have been very near for many years, but now I am still nearer, waiting for the moment to come which will be heralded by the trumpets of Michael, and the bells of Raphael. Then I will come and you will see me, O My daughters, and then your memories of past lives will arise like a torrent and you will remember many of the things which you learnt at My feet.

Man has progressed since the day I walked on your Earth, in his intelligence, and his application of scientific discoveries, but his wisdom and his love have not progressed to the same extent. He is as a labourer who knew how to sow, but who has forgotten to put in the living seed so that when the summer comes his fields are barren and he suffers the pangs of hunger.

Today man is truly hungry for what he lost since the words of My apostles died in the rituals of indifference and the greed of those who used My Church to serve Caesar instead of God. The result is the destruction and suffering you are witnessing today.

I will come through the Word. Watch for it, because you have been chosen to be among the first to hear it, with all those, who,

during their present incarnation have waited in love and in faith
for the fulfilment of the promise I made when I last parted from
this Earth.

❧❀☙

December 11th, 1956 — Prayer of the Holy Mother

You who saw me weep, gather My tears in your hands;
    Bathe your eyes in their sweetness, for in My tears there
    is no bitter salt.
Rather like honey, or like dew will you feel them
    as you take them to your face and heart.
They are the tears of womanhood, shed for the cruelty and
    blindness of man.
They are the tears of mothers, shed for the useless death
    of their sons.
Each time that I see cruelty, greed or senseless destruction,
    I shed these tears, hoping that they will melt the
    harshness and the greed.
Today I weep when I see the gift of Life so shamelessly laid
    to waste, and the sacrifice of My Son put to naught by
    those who should have been ready to bless and
    follow Him.
O let My tears blind those who want to shed their brother's
    blood, soothe those who are wounded in battle,
    melt the heart of Cain ever ready to murder Abel.
O for the sake of My Son and your Saviour listen to My voice,
    and let the gentle sound of pity cling to your devoted
    hearts, which I want to impregnate with the soothing
    gentleness of My healing powers that I hereby bestow
    on your hands if you will give your voice to the service
    of My cause.

❧❀☙

May 28th, 1957

Do not be frightened of your higher mind. It is My precious child, and it lies in My arms, so even if it were speaking to you, it would only transmit into your inner ear the thought that I gently whispered into it. This is for your reassurance.

The moment that you empty your mind of the clutter of worldly worries, personal desires, and the rush of your everyday life, the things which come into the cleansed and prepared cup, are of God, whatever the level of the sphere it has been sent from.

Imagine a radio station. Its centre of power is located in one place. It sends beams to the receiving stations, which, in turn, beam it onto other related stations, which capture the main beam. Does it mean that it captures another or a different message? No. It only means that it passes through different transmitters.

In this way you must reflect on the messages that you receive from our world. Either they come to you directly, or come through messengers, or through your own higher mind, but these different channels of transmission do not alter the nature of the message. As you go through the summer, you will receive, more and more, the feel of the source, the sense of the source. Think often of it. Think of the messages as a trans-Atlantic cable. How much would you hear without these amplifiers? The same conditions apply in the higher universe as in the physical universe. These messengers, whose vibrations are as high as those of the Dwellers of the Higher Spheres, carry the messages and amplify them for their absorption by your still-numbed inner ear.

This is a very important lesson for you. Understand well that in our world there are no miracles. Everything is clear, understandable, and logical. The only miracle and also that which is called grace, is the opening up of a direct channel to the higher spheres, an experience that can be prepared in the material world, to an explosion. But even an explosion has understandable causes. We will talk to you about this one day, as a preparation for your great experience.

Listen to the sounds of Nature and store them in your heart. This will attune you to the Universe and restore your energy by an influx of Cosmic Power. Contact with Nature is very important as there are so many things happening now which are upsetting the balance of the planet. Anyone doing psychic work and spiritual work must be renewed in the green cloak of Nature. Try to meditate on this truth and feel the current inside and the current outside circulating in spirals from earth to heaven and coming down again into your vehicles recharging them with etheric vitality.

❧❀☙

June 1957
Paris — Thalia and Ninon — through Ninon

Do not try to sort out the threads of your many lives. You will waste your time. Concentrate on the thread that you are spinning now. We do the tapestry. Give us good thread.

❧❀☙

August 24th, 1957

I was with you the whole night, working over your centres, bringing down on them the Blessing of the Holy Spirit, so that you may gradually understand your place in the Hierarchy and do the work that you pledged yourself to before you came down into your present bodies.

Only by bringing down the Holy Spirit can the disorder be made order again and the balance re-established. That is why we need the help of women like you, who can work in the world as a living sisterhood, dedicated to bringing down the Holy Spirit into the world.

We never ask impossible tasks of our students. We only want them to see the Way, and to be able to use their opportunities as they arise, as part of the work to be done. We create the opportunity. When it comes, we only want you to understand that the time has come for you to grasp it in the light of what we have taught you.

❧ ❀ ☙

August 27th, 1957

Everything which jars or grates is of the nature of Darkness in the spiritual world. Only on the right note and with the right gesture can the channel be opened and the door smoothly and silently glide into place to reveal the inner Temple. You must learn this lesson in order to go further on your way.

❧ ❀ ☙

August 30th, 1957

Thou Divine Master of Forgiveness
Give us the power to bless our enemies
And to pray that those who misuse
Thy Divine Blood
Be shown the Light
That ever shines in the inner shrine
Of Thy Temple

May the Holy Spirit come to us
In the shape of Thy Dove
That peace may reign on earth
And in the hearts of men.

❧ ❀ ☙

August 31st, 1957

In this present day and age, the danger lies not, as it did in the Middle Ages, in inhumanity and the destruction of self and others in the name of spirituality, [9] but in the trend which started after the Renaissance, of sinking into the darkness of purely materialist thinking.[10]

9.   Crusades to the Holy Land and the Albigensian Crusade against the Cathars
10. Scientific Materialism or Scientific Reductionism

The inner intention of the Crusades was to lead the dedicated knights to the wisdom of the Essenes. They made the foolish error, inspired by Rome, to fight for the grave which was empty. That is why they were led to disaster. We have to repair that mistake and find what the Crusade was really meant to find — the inner Castle of the Grail.

We, the guides between Heaven and Earth, are here to guide you in your private evolution, trying to impress you every time we can, with the lesson that is needed, the task that has to be accomplished. By using your experience, your memories, and lighting them with our wisdom, we help you on the way to a fuller work and service. We ourselves do not know the final answers to many of the questions which will only be answered in the Holiest and most distant realms. As you are infants to us, so we are infants to the Mighty Dominions and Powers and we too are learning all the time. We wanted you to know this in order to prevent any discouragement on your part.

❧❀☙

October 27th 1957
London — Thalia and Ninon — through Ninon

Please bear in mind that all systems and all techniques are imperfect, because even if divinely inspired, they can only represent a portion of the truth and that portion has to be communicated in a way that can be comprehended by the logical human mind. It is up to the individual himself to choose what crutches he needs in order to help himself on the way, until he is strong enough to throw away all crutches and communicate directly with the invisible helpers, who were sent down by what you call the Hierarchy, to help those souls who were ripe enough to take the shortcut, and to enter consciously a higher plane of existence.

Apart from the Teachings of the great World Helpers sent directly by the Father, there are no systems which can apply to all candidates groping for enlightenment. Once a human being has heard the call and become free from the fetters of material bondage, each case is different because each human being is different, having his own evolution, his own particular lesson to learn. What he has to learn is absolutely his own and does not apply to another human being.

If you distribute your energy rightly, you will find that you can do everything well and efficiently. It is when you give too much attention to some of your daily activities, that you get lost. Giving some of these too much attention and energy, confuses you and you feel depleted and frustrated. Balance is essential.

The next morning:

Yes, we have succeeded in putting you "in tune" again. A human soul is like an instrument. It is either in tune or it rings flat. When your soul is harmonious it can vibrate with all the vibrations of the spirit and take part in the wonderful concert of the universe. Then everything is easy and smooth and God's symphony from the Highest Spheres can be heard on the lowest level of the mineral world.

You do not know nor can you realise how precious in the eyes of the Son, are the souls He can use to orchestrate the symphony of the universe.

Peace is Harmony. War and destruction are discordance. In Apocalyptic times like this one, we have to rely on harmonious souls to bring down to earth the work of the angels. If your role seems menial and unimportant, it is because you still see things in a small personal way and don't realise that chalices are reduced to vases when you deprive them of their immortal content.

It is only when you face the Day of Judgement that you will see in the great mirror of Michael what you have been doing in your past life and then you will get the blissful fruits of your reward or the bitter grain of your disobedience. As long as you listen, you are doing well for your evolution and going forward.

ക്ക

February 1958
New York — Thalia, Lilla and Ninon — through Ninon

Peace be with you. Peace, peace My Blessed Daughters. It is from peace that I want to speak to you tonight because verily, verily, I say unto you, My future name will be the Peacemaker and it is as the Master of Peace that I am appearing tonight to those who are gathered in My Name throughout the world. For Peace is the Castle of shining Truth where the hidden can be revealed and the soul can don its robe of glory.

Where there is blood, greed, and hate, My Kingdom has been denied, and I am put on the Cross of shame. O you who since the beginning of My Mission have chosen to follow Me, hark well to My words. The time of My Coming is due and those who deny Me will be thrown out of My castle and plunged into the night of the soul. The way is narrow and the path is steep, and beneath them flow the waters of oblivion, from where the unfaithful will once more have to fight their way up to the Kingdom, which has been closed to them because of their blindness.

Prepare and be ready, and when the sign is given go into the world and proclaim My words so that those who have been sleeping should be awakened before the drawbridge is raised and the doors closed. Tell them, O tell them, the splendours of My castle where is served the meal of purity which changes blood into flowers and flames into jewels. This is the period of reckoning which I already described to you when we were together on the sands of Palestine.

First the call of the trumpet will be heard and you should all gather in My name, saying, "the Master is on his way." Then shall the trumpet sound a second time and you shall all fall on your knees, saying "the Master is coming". Then shall the last call be heard and you will see the Way shining in the dazzling whiteness of the Sun that never sleeps. Then all those who are ready will slowly climb to the steep top and will be together with the waiting guides and the angels to sing the Hosanna of Praise because the Mission will have been accomplished, the wound healed, and the blood will turn once more into the living waters.

But those who stayed behind will perish in the blood of their brothers and the clash of steel raised against the heavenly rainbow. Verily, verily, I say unto you, I will not come as a judge because the judgement will have taken place already, and the just and My children will be gathered in the hall. To them I will say I am the PEACEMAKER. Partake with me of the bread of Peace. For then the castle and all its dwellers will be raised with Me to the throne of the Father and the Mission will be accomplished. The Word will again dwell with God. Bear this image in mind and fear will be cast away from your soul. Be happy in My Name. As the Prince of Peace, I bless you and dedicate you once more to My service as at the time when you took your vows.

❧❀☙

Pentecost 1958
Chyknell, Shropshire [Thalia's new home]

Greetings and blessings, my children. First, a word from your dear Francis who rejoices with you today at this great Feast of the Spirit. I want to speak to you of my friends of the subhuman world, and of Nature's loneliness in a world that is receding from her at a dangerous pace. Man has become too self-important and we fear that his pride in his own creations is bound to upset the balance of the Universe at his expense.

It was our beloved Father's wish that man should learn slowly the working of His laws and discover the secrets of the house he was called to live in. It was not the plan that he should consider himself the architect and start building on his own. This may seem trivial to you but you must think further and you will discover my meaning. There is no break in God's evolution, there is no break in man's unfolding. Step-by-step, the progress is made and after a stage has been reached, the next one can come forth. What is God's is always smooth, harmonious; there is no gap, no break. But when man attempts to substitute himself for God, if he is not attuned to the Cosmic Law as it is reflected in Nature, he may create discord, disharmony, which finally expresses itself as illness — illness of the body, sickness of the mind, national and international diseases — and what are wars but outbreaks of international diseases?

All the pupils of the Holy Ones have to be healers at one time or another. The secret of healing lies in the re-establishment of harmony, by striking out the corrupting element, the false note in the mind and body or better said, in one of the subtle envelopes enveloping the human ego. The spirit, as such, is never sick. It can be paralysed, asleep — that is un-awakened — but it is never sick. The spark of the Godhead does not have within itself the element that would create sickness. It is when the spark incarnates that in one of its many garments can be found the discordant, destructive element which can strike the discordant note. It is when the negative strikes the positive or vice versa — that is, if it is not struck on the right note, to vibrate in tune with Nature, that the danger lies. Once a man understands this law properly, cancer will be cured like a simple boil. The soundness of the body is as necessary as the purity of the vehicle to contain the incarnating ego. This lesson is important and should be impressed on as many people as we can reach by those of our pupils who have the wisdom to ask us to be their guide, not relying on their own judgement as too many people do.

More and more the guidance will appear to you, and it will be, in fact, your own creation. When the pupil is wise and has learned well, his teacher wants him to become more and more creative, as this after all, is the purpose of evolution. When the vehicle is cleared, it can be trusted to receive the truth without this being dropped into it by a third agency.

❧❀☙

Pentecost, 1958

Peace be unto you, My daughters. Here I am again in your midst. You have completed the circle and you are on a higher level. You may not know it yet but you will feel it later. You have become for a moment perfectly united with Me in the Word of Truth — the Word which shall never be spoken by human lips as it is the Word of the Pure Spirit.

At this moment you have entered consciously the ranks of the Pilgrims of Light who are slowly proceeding towards the castle where the Secret Cup is hidden. You may not yet be allowed to contemplate it in your waking consciousness, but at night from now on whenever you asked one of My messengers, you will be able to go there and meet in the Hall of Learning all those kindred spirits you have always desired to contact. More and more the veil of your personality is being torn down and you are going back to your Essence and finding in her your Eternal Body of Light.

I am the Master of Compassion. What does compassion mean? It means the total release from the control of ego because you feel, endure and live with everything that in this world has been born of the Breath of the Spirit. Witness your new birth, dearest daughters, and be welcomed in the Kingdom of the Dove where lies illumined the centre of the Heart.

It is wrong to confuse personality with individuality as they are two completely different aspects of the total being. The Son of Man has shown the individual way back to the Father Godhead.

Personality [when controlled by ego] is division, separateness and illusion — Maya as My Brothers of the East call it; but individuality is the purpose of evolution, otherwise God the Father, My Father, would have remained alone in his aloof contemplation of the universe which he brought forth from His Universal Mind. Be unique by being all the others and yourself as well. This is the Law of Compassion which I brought to the world when I came down 2000 years ago.

Have you thought this is truly My anniversary as the cycle has been completed and I am being reborn as those who are with Me are being called again to do the same work but on a new level. That is why this incarnation is so important for you all as it is the final examination. As babes you came into My arms. As adults we must meet again and you will bring the fruits of your many trials and tell Me, "Master, we have not slept, but have worked and toiled for your good name. See here we bring these testimonies to you and we are weary but humbly satisfied that we did not fail in our task."

And then I will tell you that you have travelled far but you have come to the harbour at last and sitting at My feet you will hear what you have not heard before, as it was right and willed that your evolution should follow the Cup, but now from the East comes the Bright Star of the New Awakening, and I will tell you how I too had to be taught the story of those who came before Me, not from the Father but from the Great Mother. To teach the dispensation I had to go behind the walls [Tibet] and see the story of Creation, not as it is written in heaven — that I knew — but as it is written on Earth which I had come to liberate through Compassion.

You are all meant to work for unity and understanding. All the great prophets have been heralding the moment which is truly the moment of judgement of which I spoke to My disciples at the beginning of this cycle. Verily, verily, I say unto you, receive My Blessings, receive My Dove, because now Unity has to become the Law of the Earth and those who respect it and make it their own will enter with Me the Kingdom of Heaven. The others will be thrown to the bottom of the evolutionary ladder and will have to start again from the animal kingdom.

There is no place for half-men or sleeping men any more. Either you are a whole man or no man at all.

Dearest daughters, I have spoken My message of Pentecost. Peace be with you. Keep it in your heart as the glow of blood which was made to flower to redeem the Law.

❧❀☙

January 15th, 1965

We have lived for 2000 years in an Age which can be compared to adolescence. Now humanity is ready to become adult or to sink into general criminality which will bring about chaos, confusion, and final destruction. But if enough of our warriors come together and overcome the danger, we will indeed have the millennium of peace and happiness. If humanity chooses adulthood and responsibility to life, it will have the millennium of peace and happiness and Earth, in serene unity, will join the circle of planets which have already completed their evolution and have reached the state of Paradise — Paradise being the state of completed evolution where human beings, through their own decision, will have regained the angelic state.

Now the Plan is to unite East and West to achieve the Cosmic Union which is the purpose of the Age we have entered: the Liberation of the Universal with the Redemption of the Individual. This balance is one of the most difficult balances to achieve, yet it is so written in the Book of Law — that now is the time. The alternative is total destruction and annihilation for the planet which has denied its teachers. Let us call upon the Moon and the Sun, symbol of the balance to make wise the humble and humble the wise, unifying the spirit and strengthening the Sons of Man so that the Sons of God can again inhabit the Earth and make it like the original Paradise created by the Father of All in honour of His Divine Partner — the Universal Mother.

❧❀☙

Extracts of particular importance

There are periods which seem to last forever. These are periods of incubation; everything is waiting; although the dice have been thrown, the pieces have not been moved. Man is on the threshold of his greatest trial since the day of My coming. This is the time when My teaching has to be fully understood. Humanity has lived for two thousand years in a state of adolescence. Now it must become adult or sink into general criminality that will bring chaos, confusion and, finally, destruction. If humanity chooses adulthood and responsibility to life, it will have the millennium of peace and happiness and Earth will join the circle of planets which have already completed their evolution.

Everywhere on this planet the call has gone out. From far distant realms in the universe come Great Beings to your poor benighted planet to stand with the children of the Light in their effort to overthrow the tyranny of evil once and for all so that never again shall it overpower the world. If enough people stand with the Light when the darkness would engulf it, then with this help from the Cosmos, you will succeed in overcoming the darkness. But there is a danger that many will be intimidated into weak compromise or indifference. You need to become as wise as serpents and as gentle as doves.

The breaking up of the established churches is but a question of time and will be accomplished partly by their inability to satisfy the spiritual needs of man and partly by the atheists [materialists] who will play a greater and greater part in world events. Harmony must be found at every level as Man can no longer survive the disintegration of his psyche caused by his own destructive civilization. Only those who have reached an inner harmony between their knowledge and their intuition, their thoughts and their actions; those who are able to listen to and accept the guidance of their heart, will be given the strength and the knowledge to help their fellow men. It is through the intuition of the weak that the Light will be found again, not through the will of the strong.

You must find your way to the Holy Mountain [an inner state] and there prepare the teaching of the New Age when all religions will become one religion. From the centre within yourself you must radiate outward in ever growing strength until your sphere of influence has spread to include many longing and searching souls. But before this ideal is attained, the centre of yourself must be cared for and made strong. The stronger your centre, the further will the Light spread. You must only teach what you know and understand. Those who are dedicated to assisting the incarnation of heavenly things in time and space must give great care to the vehicle the soul works with — the body. Strengthen it by every means possible to carry the weight of the spirit.

Man has progressed in his intelligence and his mastery of the scientific discoveries, but his wisdom and love have not progressed to the same extent. He is as the labourer who knew how to sow but who has forgotten to put in the living seed so that when harvest comes his fields are barren and he suffers the pangs of hunger. Today man is truly hungry for what he lost since the words of My apostles died in the rituals of indifference and the greed of those who used My Church to serve Caesar instead of God. The result is the destruction and suffering you are witnessing today.

Only when men learn not to shed their brother's blood can the House of God be built on its true foundations. Either you awaken now to spiritual life or you become diseased and more or less insane. Wake up to your immortal soul or it will be taken away from you for you must know that souls can be taken away from unworthy carriers.

Humanity in its majority is still thinking in terms of the past; that is why it cannot cope with the present and still less with the future. Verily, verily, I say unto you, do not mind the temptations and seeds of the past but look up at the stars and wait for the vision that will entrance your sight and make your spirit tremble with a shaking joy.

The Divine Mother is the Holy Spirit who presides over the New Age. Inspired by her, women, through their love and understanding, have been given the task of awakening in men the compassion and devotion to life taught by Me at the beginning of the Piscean Age. Man through woman, will realise in himself the sense of his mission on earth and see clearly as in a mirror, the Law of the Universe. When that time comes, the secrets of Nature will be understood.

Do not offend Nature. Do not offend God by tampering with the laws of Nature, trying to bend them to your destructive purposes. Every act of a human being must be judged according to the rule: Does it offend Nature? Does it offend God? Does it injure Life?

If man uses his control of Nature for love and for blessing, this Aquarian Age will be the fulfilment of My coming. The universe is changing and the cosmic rays which strike your planet are now potent with the power to create or destroy. The choice is man's: will he choose to be the Son or the Rebel?

We may witness another catastrophe unless we call on the Divine Mother to help us to receive the influx of power coming with the New Age. There will be crisis after crisis that will completely upset the human mind and split the frame of civilization. The wanton thirst to kill will be roused more and more. For no logical reason blood is being shed and more will follow. Pray that you be given the strength to resist the madness that will be the fourth horseman of these times.

It was our beloved Father's wish that man should learn slowly the working of His laws and discover the secrets of the house he was called to live in. It was not the plan that he should consider himself the architect and start building on his own.

There will be greater and more terrible discoveries than the splitting of the atom. More devastating weapons are being worked upon in secret, weapons so powerful that they can reverse the laws of Nature. Already you see the results around you of man's presumptuous endeavour to use the elements of matter, not for beneficial purposes but to destroy life. Destructive energy emanates from places where scientists are working to develop new weapons. This energy affects human bodies and human minds, creating split psyches which are the equivalent on the human plane of what the splitting of energy is on the cosmic plane. There is a danger of collective insanity.

If you mix the waters of knowledge with the thought of destruction, destruction will come. The control of Nature now nearly acquired can be used for love and blessing or for malediction and hate.

The Age of Aquarius is the Age of Hydrogen where hydrogen may mean the destruction of this planet or its trans-formation into the true Elysium. It would be better for those of this generation never to have been born, than having been born, not to become fully awakened to the moral responsibility of this dangerous yet promise-fulfilling age.

You must be aware of the danger to the waters of the world created by atomic explosions. The Holy Mother weeps over the profanation and pollution of her healing waters. Her tears fall as crystals on your souls, striving to awaken them to the understanding of the great threat to Nature caused by these explosions. Listen to the despairing voice of your Mother, the Earth. Only by the raising of your consciousness to the realisation of the Oneness of life can you escape destruction and acquire the wisdom rightly to use the power that your intelligence has given you over Nature. Scientific knowledge must be raised to the level of this realisation. Blessed are those who see behind and beyond the veils of separateness to the Divine Unity of all life.

You are all meant to work for unity and understanding. You can, by concentration, meditation and the humility of prayer, learn to use the force of blessing in your words, your gestures, your writings, your approach to other human beings and to all other species. All the great prophets have been heralding the moment which is truly the moment of judgement of which I spoke to My disciples at the beginning of this cycle.

Verily, verily, I say unto you, receive My blessings, receive My Dove, because now unity has to become the law of the earth and those who respect it and make it their own will enter with me the Kingdom of Heaven. The others will be thrown to the bottom of the evolutionary ladder and will have to start again from the animal kingdom. There is no place for half men or sleeping men any more. Either you are a full man or you are no man at all.

The Plan is now to melt East and West to achieve the cosmic union which is the purpose of the age we have entered: the liberation of the Universal with the redemption of the individual. The balance is one of the most difficult balances to achieve and yet it is so written in the Book of the Law — that now is the time; the alternative is total destruction and annihilation for the planet which has denied its teachers.

My death and resurrection were meant to help man to realise his lasting power to survive death and to achieve his salvation through devotion to his fellow men. It is necessary for man to know there is no death for the soul.

Think often of the Source. Feel the presence of it. Think of its messengers and the amplifiers of the message. Learn to express in your own time and space what is eternal, indivisible and holy. You should no more lead an ill-fitted life than wear an ill-fitting garment. Learn to divide your time between the duties of your daily life and those of your inner self and give them your undivided attention.

Create gardens to protect the purity of Nature from all destructive rays. Protect the birds. Tell other people about angels. Make the stars weep for joy. Your channels can be blocked through grief and doubt. Throw doubt away in the name of Christ. Build a wall of light around you when you paint, speak or write. Do not try to sort out the threads of your many lives. You will waste your time. Concentrate on the thread you are spinning now. We do the tapestry. Give us good thread.

All systems and techniques are imperfect because, even if divinely inspired, they can only present a portion of the truth. It is up to the individual to choose what crutches he needs until he is strong enough to throw them away and communicate directly with the invisible helpers who are sent down to help those souls who are ready to enter consciously into a higher plane of existence.

A human soul is like an instrument. It is tuned or it rings flat. You do not know how precious are, in the eyes of the Son, the souls He can use to orchestrate the symphony of the universe.

Keep knocking and gently, very gently the door will open so that you will have time to prepare and bear the radiance of the vision that will fill your mind with the realisation of the immortal truth. Each day, each minute is a preparation. Only through awareness and longing from you to Me can I bring you the blessing of the millennium. When the light comes, it is all the more luminous because of the darkness that has gone before.

The only miracle and what is called grace is the opening up of a direct channel to the Higher Spheres: an experience that can be compared in the material world to an explosion. Only on the right note and with the right gesture can the channel be opened and the door glide into place to reveal the inner Temple.

Do not despair over your lack of achievement. It only needs a few years, days or hours of complete realisation and service in one incarnation to make worthwhile the eternal spiral and your arduous way back to the heavenly spheres.

❧ ❀ ☙

A Final Word:

I have brought together these Messages in memory and in love for my mother and love for the Higher Assembly of Beings who watch over the life of this planet. They have been the foundation and the inspiration of all my own work. May they reach those who can assimilate their teaching and take it further. Their words are witness to the fact that we do not live in a dead, insentient universe that is without consciousness, purpose or meaning. On the contrary, we live in a universe that is alive, sentient, full of wonders, peopled with countless beings in higher dimensions, as well as in other galaxies and on other planets — all directed by an evolutionary intention.

Anne Baring

Love be with you.
Love be with the world.
Love be the only eternal blessing.